LOCAL RED BOOK

KIDLINGTON

EYNSHAM · WHEATLEY · WOODSTOCK

CONTENTS

Page Layout & Road Map   **2**
2½ Miles to 1 Inch

Oxford Enlarged Centre   **4-5**
8 Inches to 1 Mile

Street Maps   **3-27**
4 Inches to 1 Mile

Index to Streets   **27**

Redbooks showing the way

ery effort has been made to verify the accuracy of information in this book but the blishers cannot accept responsibility for expense or loss caused by an error or omission.

'ormation that will be of assistance to the user of the maps will be welcomed.

e representation on these maps of a road, track or path is no evidence of the existence of a ht of way.

'eet plans prepared and published by ESTATE PUBLICATIONS, Bridewell House, NTERDEN, KENT. The Publishers acknowledge the co-operation of the local authorities of vns represented in this atlas.

Cartography by Craig Gibson

Ordnance Survey® This product includes mapping data licensed from Ordnance Survey® with the permission of the Controller of Her Majesty's Stationery Office.

'Crown Copyright   All rights reserved
Estate Publications 333-06   ISBN 1 84192 305 2   Licence number 100019031

www.ESTATE-PUBLICATIONS.co.uk

Printed by Ajanta Offset, New Delhi, India.

LEGEND

▬▬▬	Motorway
▬▬	'A' Road
▬▬	'B' Road
═══	Minor Road
▨▨▨	Pedestrianized / Restricted Access
═══	Track
	Built Up Area
- - - - -	Footpath
∿∿	Stream
∿∿	River
Lock	Canal
▬■▬	Railway / Station
●	Post Office
P P+☐	Car Park / Park & Ride
C	Public Convenience
+	Place of Worship
→	One-way Street
i	Tourist Information Centre
▲8 ▲8	Adjoining Pages
	Area Depicting Enlarged Centre
	Emergency Services
	Industrial Buildings
	Leisure Buildings
	Education Buildings
	Hotels etc.
	Retail Buildings
	General Buildings
	Woodland
	Recreation Ground
	Cemetery

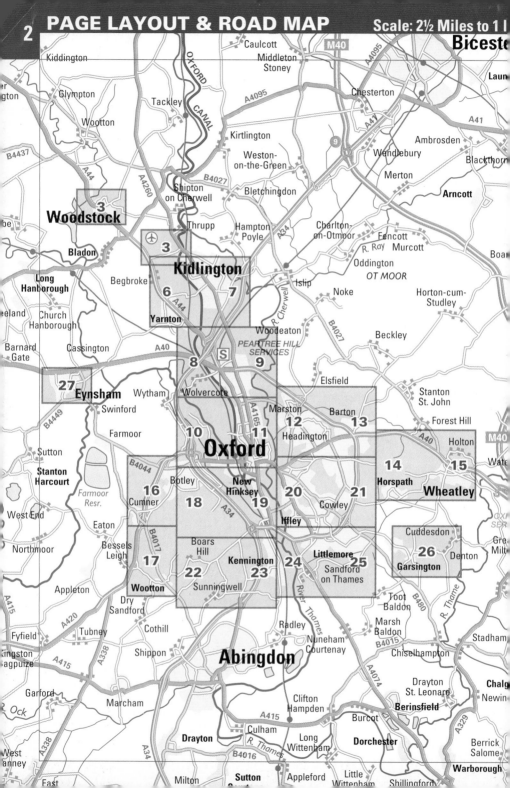

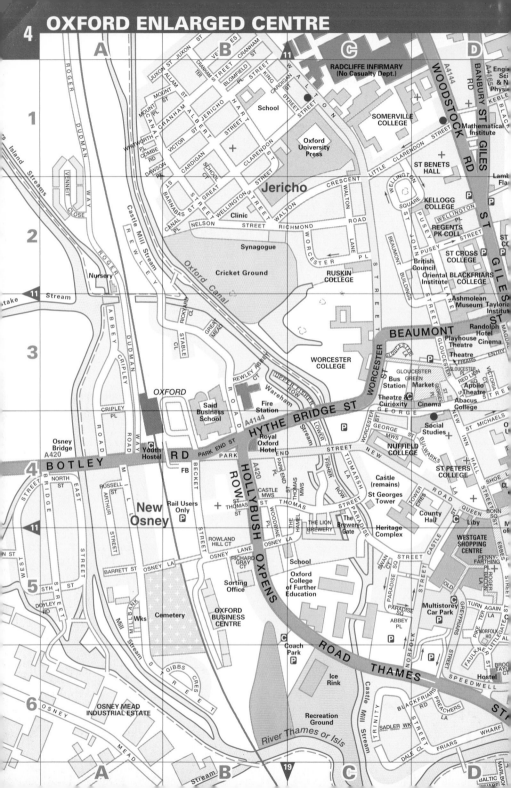

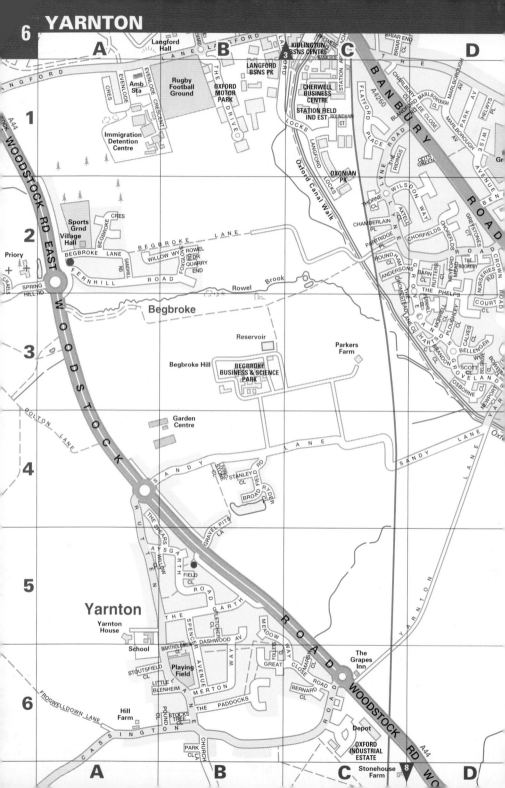

Langford Hall

A

LANGFORD LANE

B

KIDLINGTON BSNS CENTRE

C

FRIAR END

THE

D

LANGFORD

Rugby Football Ground

OXFORD MOTOR PARK

LANGFORD BSNS PK

CHERWELL BUSINESS CENTRE

STATION FIELD IND EST

BANKSIDE

CHARLBURY

MARLBOROUGH

A4260

MARLBOROUGH AV

WISE AVENUE

PARK AV

HELWYS PL

EVENLODE CRES

Amb Sta

THE OXFORD

BLANDFORD AV

MARLBOROUGH

BEN

Gr

EVENLODE CRESCENT

Immigration Detention Centre

1

DRIVE

Roundham CT

STATION ROAD

LYNE ROAD

FLATFORD

PLACE

THE RIDINGS

COTS GREEN

CROWN

WOODSTOCK RD EAST

A44

BEGBROKE CRES

Sports Grnd Village Hall

SANDHILL RD

BEGBROKE LANE

WILLOW WY

FERNHILL ROAD

BEGBROKE LANE

ROWEL DR

FOXGLOVE

QUARRY END

OXONIAN PK

OXFORD CANAL WALK

LANGFORD LOCKS

THORNE CL

CHAMBERLAIN PL

PARTRIDGE

WILSDON WAY

AXTELL

ROUND HAM CL

ANDERSONS

BARN CL

GROVE

MORRELL CL

GREYSTONES

CHORFIELDS

CHORFIELDS

MEYFORD

THE PHELPS

NURSERIES

THE ROOKERY

COURT CL

2

Priory

CHAELS

SPRING HILL RD

ROAD

Brook

Rowel

Rowel Brook

THE HOMESTEAD LANE CL

RUTTERS

PLOUGHLEY

HARBRANDON CL

CALVES

BELLENGER

SCOTT CL

BELGROVE

WY

NEWPORT CL

3

Begbroke

Reservoir

Begbroke Hill

BEGBROKE BUSINESS & SCIENCE PARK

Parkers Farm

GROVELANDS

OSBORNE

BOXHILL

Garden Centre

WOODSTOCK

DOLTON LANE

SANDY

LANE

SANDY LANE

LANE

Ox

4

RUTTEN

LIME WALK

STANLEY CL

BROAD FIELD RD

RYDER

LANE

GRAVEL PITS LA

5

Yarnton

Yarnton House

School

THE SPEARS

AYSGARTH

WILLOW

FIELD CL

ROAD GARTH

GARTH

THE

SPENCER

GRETCHENROD

DASHWOOD AV

AVENUE

MEADOW WAY

FULLER

CLOSE

YARNTON

The Grapes Inn

6

FROGWELLDOWN LANE

Hill Farm

CASSINGTON

Playing Field

BARTHOLOMEW CL

STOUTSFIELD

LITTLE BLENHEIM

POUND

STOCKS TREE CL

PARK CL

CHURCH LANE

THE PADDOCKS

MERTON

BERNARD

GREAT

CLOSE

MARSH

ROAD

ROAD

WOODSTOCK ROAD

Depot

OXFORD INDUSTRIAL ESTATE

Stonehouse Farm

8

A44

WO

A

B

C

D

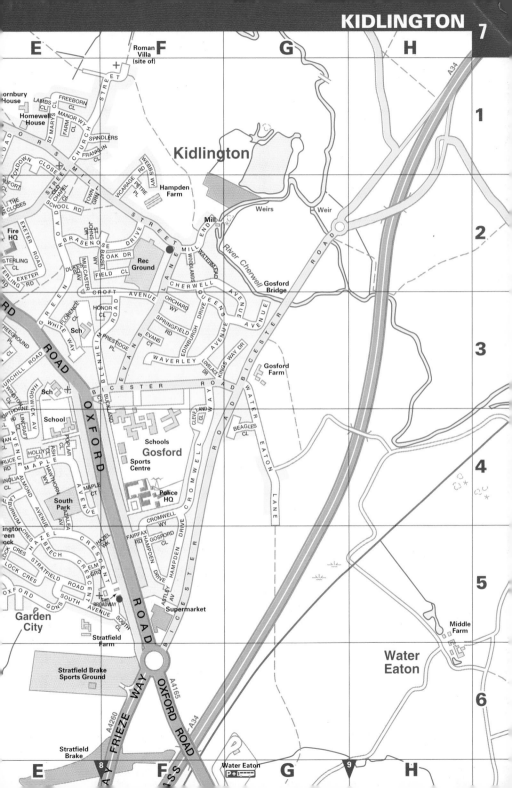

E 7 F G H 9

1

2

St Frideswide
Farm

River Cherwell

3

Cutteslowe

Sports
Ground

HASLEMERE
GDNS

Cutteslowe
Park

Sescut
Farm

TALBOT
RD

HAYWARD ROAD

HARBORD ROAD

PARK CL

PENNYWELL
DR

Sports
Ground

Cutteslowe
Park House

LOVELACE SQ

LOVE LA

TEMPLAR
RD

MILLERS
ACRE

MARRIOTT
CL

BOURNE
CL

KENDAL CRES

SPARSEY
PL

HAREFIELDS

DELL

DAVID WALTER CL

PRIORS
FORGE

HOLT WEER CL

4

ELSFIELD

HAWKSMOOR
SUNNYMEAD
CT

PRIORY
RD

JACKSON RD

WYATT RD

School

Community
Centre

BANBURY ROAD

WAY

Cherwell
Farm

NORTHERN

CARLTON ROAD

WOLSEY

SOUTHDALE RD

CAVENDISH RD

BODLEY
PL

BUCKLER PL

SCOTT RD

WERM RD

Sunnymead
Recreation
Ground

Cherwell
Bridge

New Manor
Farm

Hill
Farm

MILL LANE

PLAND
CT

ND PARK RD

ROAD

WENTWORTH ROAD

SALISBURY RD

ALDRICH ROAD

WATER EATON RD

HAPSLEY ROAD

MULBERRY
CT

THE PADDOX

PADDOX CL

SQUITCHEY LANE

CAPEL CL

HERNES CRES

HERNES ROAD

HEATHON RD

LIP
ROAD

ISLIP
PL

WEST
GRO

HARPES ROAD

LUCERNE RD

Sunnymead

BY-PASS

12

Sch

RICHARDS LA

SUMMERHILL CT

VICTORIA ROAD

KINGS CROSS ROAD

HAMILTON ROAD

HAWKSWELL
GDNS

River Cherwell

Hill View
Farm

BISHOP
KIRK PL

HOBSON RD

HYDE
PL

GROVE ST

PORTLAND ROAD

OSBERTON RD

WOODSTOCK RD

RIDGEMONT

Rec
Grnd

Sch

CYPERS ST

ROGERS ST

BBC
Radio
Oxford

Liby

SOUTH PARADE

LONSDALE RD

MAYFIELD RD

School

Swimming
Pool

Summertown

Victoria
Arms

CUMBERLE CL

WARDS

AV

A4144

ROAD

A4165

SUMMERFIELD RD

STRATFIELD

DIAMC

EWERT

Oxford Delegacy of
Local Examinations

Northern Meadow
Farm

School

ng Fields

E

F 11

The Cherwell
School

G

H

THORPE ROAD

The Ferry
Centre

Playing
Field

Mar

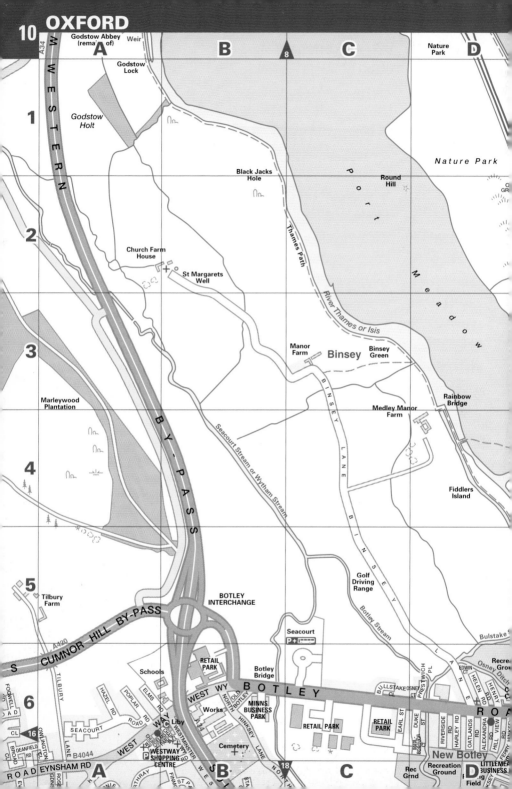

A34
WESTERN

Godstow Abbey
(rema' of)
Weir
A
B
8
C
Nature
Park
D

Godstow
Lock

Godstow
Holt

1

Nature Park

Black Jacks
Hole
Round
Hill
Po
r
t

2

Thames Path

Church Farm
House

St Margarets
Well

River Thames or Isis

M
e
a
d
o
w

Manor
Farm
Binsey
Binsey
Green

3

Marleywood
Plantation

B
-
Y
-
P
A
S
S

Seacourt Stream or Wytham Stream

B
I
N
S
E
Y

L
A
N
E

Medley Manor
Farm

Rainbow
Bridge

4

Fiddlers
Island

B
I
N
S
E
Y

Golf
Driving
Range

Botley Stream

L
A

5
Tilbury
Farm

BOTLEY
INTERCHANGE

Seacourt
P+

Bulstake

A420
CUMNOR HILL BY-PASS
S
TILBURY

RETAIL
PARK

Schools

Botley
Bridge

Recre
Osney Ditch Gro

BULLSTAKE
OSNEY
CL

PRESTWICH
PL

EDWIN
CT

ALEXANDRA
RD
HELEN
RD

R O
A

6

WEST WY

OLD
BOTLEY
NORTH

B O T L E Y

EARL
ST

RIVERSIDE
RD

DUKE
ST
HARLEY
RD

HENRY
RD

Works
MINNS
BUSINESS
PARK

RETAIL PARK
RETAIL
PARK

OATLANDS
RD

HILL VIEW
RD

R O A

HAZEL
RD

POPLAR
RD
ELMS
RD

WEST
WAY

Liby
HINKSEY
LANE

FOGWELL
RD
E
V
A
D

CL
16
DEANFIELD
RD

SEACOURT
LANE

WESTMINSTER
WAY

WEST
WAY

WESTWAY
SHOPPING
CENTRE

Cemetery

New Botley
LITTLEMC
BUSINESS

Rec
Grnd
Recreation
Ground
Field

R O A D
EYNSHAM RD
B4044
A
B
18
NORTH
C
D

E   F   G   H

1

B4027

Holton Wood

Red Hill

Warren Farm

Warren Wood

Pond Farm

Old Park Farm

2

Lyehill Quarries (disused)

Buryhook Corner

Warwick Close Farm

Cottage Copse

Hill House

Recreation Ground

School

Holton

Holton Place

The Rectory

3

Liby

The Park Sports Centre

School

Moat

Playing Field

Church Farm

Garden Copse

OXFORD BROOKES UNIVERSITY

COLLEGE CL

PARK HILL ROAD

WESTFIELD

Club

Wheatley Centre

Sch

BLENHEIM ROAD

KILN CL

GARDINER CL

TEMPLARS CL

MORLAND CL

ST MARYS CL

HOLLOWAY RD

THE GLEBE

N DON

FAIRFAX GATE

BSNS CENTRE

TYNDALE PL

4

LITTLEWORTH

BARLOW CL

BEECHING WY

HOPE

Littleworth Mobile Park

TTLEWORTH BUSINESS CENTRE

HIGH ROAD

CHURCH ROAD

Liby

Sch

HIGH HAYS

FARM CLOSE

STREET

ROAD

MULBERRY DR

FRIDAYS

CROWN ROAD

OLD THE TRIANGLE

SANDHILL

Fire Sta

LONDON RD

THE AVENUE

Garden Centre

ROAD

A40

5

SIMONS CL

HOWE CL

KELHAM

STATION

CLIMBER

HALL

COOMBE

DR

BEECH ROAD

ORCHARD CL

JACKIES LA

ELM CL

HILARY WY

ROMAN

AMBROSE RISE

LEYSHON RD

GULLUM HO

CULLUM RD

MILLER RD

ELTON CRES

THE AVENUE

Works

Sewage Works

WINDMILL LANE

LANE HILL

LADDER LANE

Coombe House

Castle Hill Farm

6

Coombe Wood

New Barn

E   F   G   H

Wheatley

Map labels

A **B** **C** **D**

1

B4044
EYNSHAM ROAD
A420
BY-PASS

Cammoor Copse
Stimpsons Cottages
Stimpsons Copse

HOMESTALL RD
FOGWELL RD
POTTLE CL
STONE CL
BUSHEY
LONG CL
ASHCROFT CL

2

Red House Farm

Nobles
Tudor Court Park Home Estate
Oxford Hearing Centre

EYNSHAM
STIMPSONS CL
FOGWELL CT
GRANGE CT
FOGWELL RD

Dean Court
NOBLES CL
GREEN LA
PINNOCKS CL
WAY
WAY
THIRD ACRE RISE
QUEENS CL
PINNOCKS
DEANS RD
MIKA PL
DEAN COURT RD
ARNOLDS

Denmans Farm
ORCHARD
DENTON CL
STUBBLETON
BROWNS CL

3

Denmans Copse

Saddle Copse

HILL

Hids Copse

HIDS COPSE RD
HIDS
HIDS COPSE RD
THE CEDARS
DELAMARE
BARN CL
Cumnor Hill
COTSWOLD
TURNPIKE RD
DELAMARE CL
LANE

4

Nursery

Longmoor Brake
CHAWLEY
Well Yard Copse
Long Copse
Chawley Farm
COG GROVE DOWN
HILLSIDE
DOWN
HURST

5

ge RD

B4017
HIGH
College Farm
School
DENMANS LA
SANDS CL
STREET
OXFORD RD
ABINGDON RD
OXFORD RD
NORREYS ROAD
NORREYS ROAD
BERTIE ROAD
ROAD
CUMNOR
LANE
HILL
Chawley
Timber Yard

Cumnor
APPLETON RD
GLEBE RD
THE GLEBE
OXENFORD RD
Cumnor Folly
Hurst Hill

6

ng d

THE WINNYARDS
Playing Field
THE PARK
KENILWORTH RD
FORSTER RD
ROBSART RD
ROBSART PL
ABINGDON ROAD
Cross Roads Farm
B4017
A420

A **B** **C** **D**

17

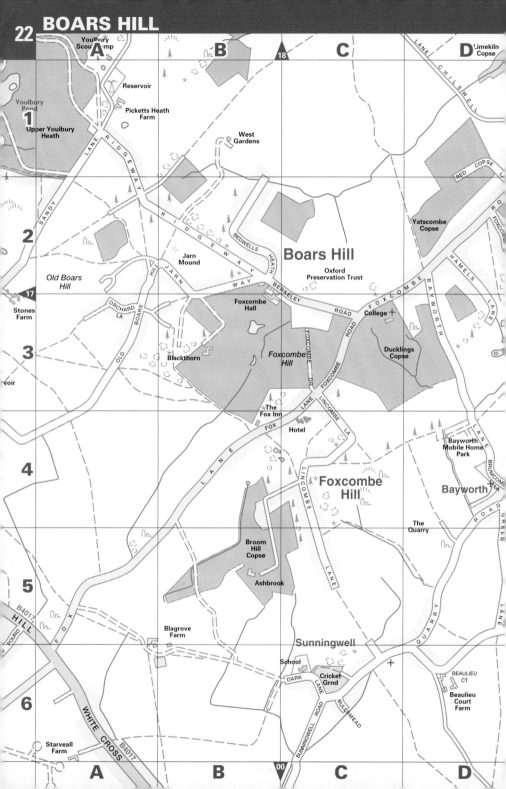

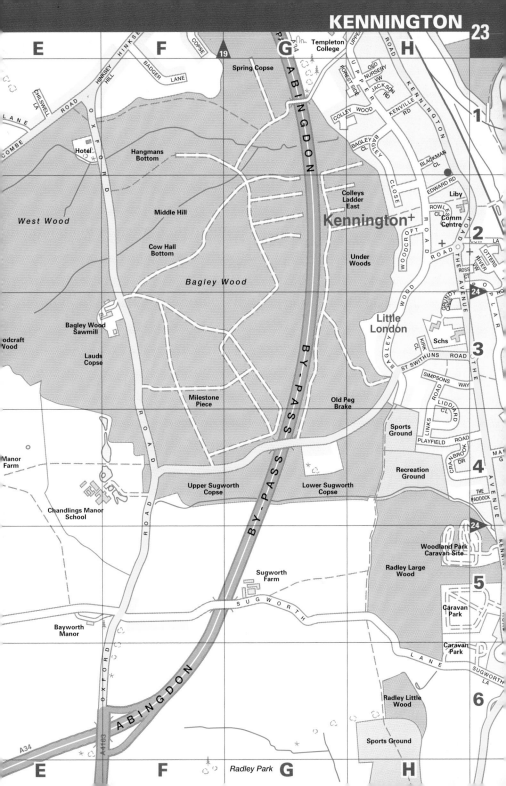

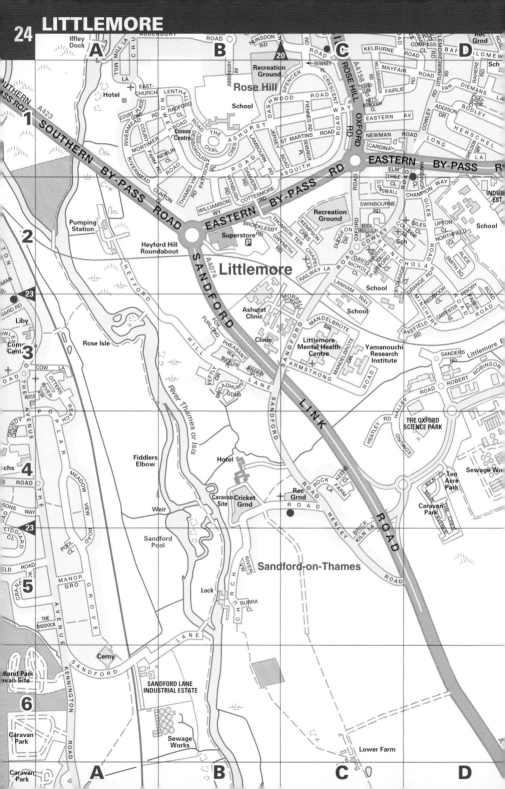

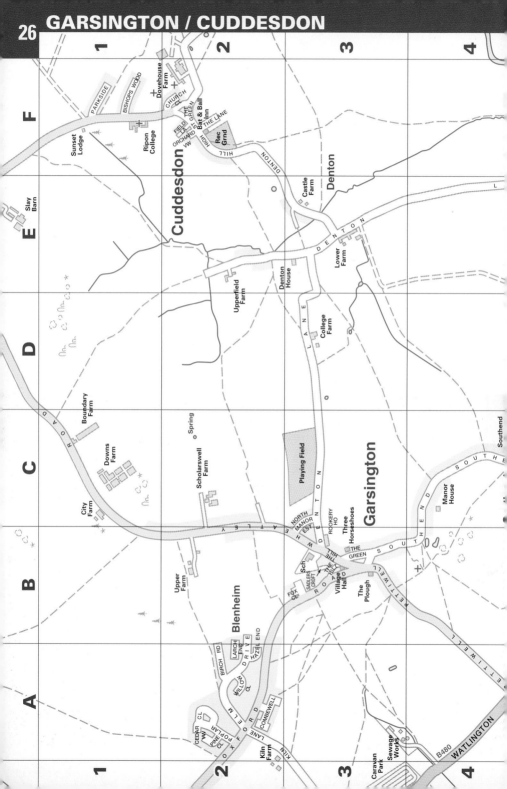

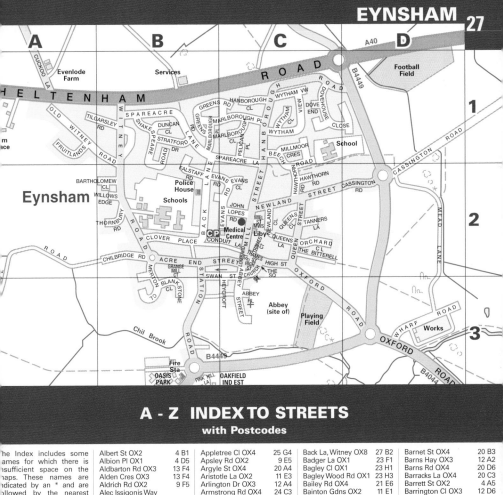

A - Z INDEX TO STREETS
with Postcodes

The Index includes some names for which there is insufficient space on the maps. These names are indicated by an * and are followed by the nearest adjoining thoroughfare.

Abberbury Av OX4 24 B1
Abberbury Rd OX4 20 A6
Abbey Pl,
Oxford OX1 4 C5
Abbey Pl,
Witney OX8 27 C3
Abbey Rd OX2 4 A3
Abbey St OX8 27 C2
Abbots Wood East OX3 21 F3
Abbots Wood West OX3 21 F3
Abingdon By-Pass OX1 19 G6
Abingdon Rd,
Cumnor OX2 16 A5
Abingdon Rd,
Oxford OX1 19 G2
Ablett Cl OX4 20 B2
Acacia Av OX4 25 F3
Acland Cl OX3 20 D1
Acre Cl OX3 21 F3
Acre End St OX8 27 B2
Acremead Rd OX33 14 D5
Addison Cres OX4 20 A4
Addison Dr OX4 24 D1
Adelaide St OX2 11 E4
Admiral Cl OX4 25 F4
Agnes Ct OX4 20 D4

Albert St OX2 4 B1
Albion Pl OX1 4 D5
Aldbarton Rd OX3 13 F4
Alden Cres OX3 13 F4
Aldrich Rd OX2 9 F5
Alec Issigonis Way OX4 21 E5
Alesworth Gro OX3 12 C3
Alexandra Cts*,
Middle Way OX2 9 E6
Alexandra Rd OX2 10 D6
Alfred St OX1 5 E4
Alice Smith Sq OX4 24 D2
All Saints Rd OX3 12 D6
Allam St OX2 4 B1
Allan Bullock Cl*,
Caroline St OX4 20 A1
Allin Cl OX4 25 F1
Alma Pl OX4 20 A2
Almond Av OX5 7 E4
Ambassador Av OX4 25 F1
Ambleside Dr OX3 12 C3
Ambrose Rise OX33 15 G4
Amey Cres OX13 17 D6
Amory Cl OX4 25 E1
Anchor Ct OX4 5 H5
Andersons Cl OX5 6 C2
Andromeda Cl OX4 25 F3
Anemone Cl OX4 25 F4
Angel Ct*,
St Clements St OX4 20 A2
Angelica Cl OX4 25 G3
Anne Greenwood Cl OX4 20 B6
Annesley Rd OX4 20 C6
Anson Cl OX33 15 G4
Appleton Rd OX2 16 A5

Appletree Cl OX4 25 G4
Apsley Rd OX2 9 E5
Argyle St OX4 20 A4
Aristotle La OX2 11 E3
Arlington Dr OX3 12 A4
Armstrong Rd OX4 24 C3
Arnold Rd OX4 20 A4
Arthray Rd OX2 18 A1
Arnolds Way OX2 16 D3
Arthur Evans Cl OX13 17 C6
Arthur Garrard Cl OX2 11 F4
Arthur St OX2 4 A4
Ash Cl OX5 7 E4
Ash Gro OX3 13 E4
Ashcroft Cl OX2 16 D1
Ashlong Rd OX3 12 B3
Ashmole Pl OX4 25 G1
Ashurst Way OX4 24 B1
Ashville Way OX4 25 G1
Aspen Sq OX4 25 F4
Asquith Rd OX4 24 C1
Astley Av OX5 7 F5
Aston St OX4 20 A3
Atkinson Cl OX3 13 F3
Atkyns Rd OX3 21 F2
Atwell Pl OX3 21 E1
Aubrey Cl OX4 20 B6
Avens Way OX4 25 F3
Avenue La OX4 20 A2
Avery Ct OX2 9 F5
Awgar Stone Rd OX3 21 F3
Axtell Cl OX5 6 C2
Aysgarth Rd OX5 6 A5
Azalea Av OX4 7 E4
Azors Ct OX4 20 B6

Back La, Oxford OX3 12 A2

Back La, Witney OX8 27 B2
Badger La OX1 23 F1
Bagley Cl OX1 23 H1
Bagley Wood Rd OX1 23 H3
Bailey Rd OX4 21 E6
Bainton Gdns OX2 11 E1
Bainton Rd OX2 11 E2
Baker Cl OX3 13 G6
Bakers La OX4 20 A6
Balfour Rd OX4 25 F2
Balliol Ct OX2 11 E3
Baltic Wharf OX1 19 F1
Bampton Cl OX4 25 E2
Banbury Rd,
Kidlington OX5 6 C1
Banbury Rd,
Oxford OX2 4 D1
Banbury Rd,
Thrupp OX5 3 C4
Banbury Rd,
Wolvercote OX2 9 E3
Banbury Rd,
Woodstock OX20 3 C1
Banjo Rd OX4 20 D6
Bankside,
Kidlington OX5 3 D6
Bankside,
Wootton OX1 17 C4
Bankside Cl OX3 13 F5
Bannister Cl OX4 20 A3
Bardwell Ct OX2 11 G3
Bardwell Rd OX2 11 F3
Barleycott La OX1 19 F5
Barlow Cl OX33 15 E4
Barn Cl,
Kidlington OX5 6 D2
Barn Cl, Oxford OX2 16 D4

Barnet St OX4 20 B3
Barns Hay OX3 12 A2
Barns Rd OX4 20 D6
Barracks La OX4 20 C3
Barrett St OX2 4 A5
Barrington Cl OX3 12 D6
Bartholomew Cl,
Kidlington OX5 6 B6
Bartholomew Cl,
Witney OX8 27 A2
Bartholomew Rd OX4 20 D6
Bartlemas Cl OX4 20 C3
Bartlemas Rd OX4 20 B3
Barton La OX3 13 E4
Barton Rd OX3 13 F4
Barton Village Rd OX3 13 F3
Basset Way OX5 7 F2
Bassett Rd OX3 13 G4
Bateman St OX3 13 E6
Bath Pl OX1 5 F3
Bath St OX4 20 A1
Bay Tree Cl OX4 20 B6
Bayswater Farm Rd OX3 13 H4
Bayswater Rd OX3 13 G4
Bayworth La OX1 22 D2
Beagles Cl OX5 7 G4
Bear Cl OX20 3 C2
Bear La OX1 5 E4
Bears Hedge OX4 20 B6
Beauchamp La OX4 20 D6
Beauchamp Pl OX4 20 D6
Beaulieu Ct OX13 22 D6
Beaumont Bldgs OX1 4 C2
Beaumont Rd OX3 13 G5

Beaumont St OX1	4 C3
Becket St OX1	4 B4
Bedford St OX4	20 A4
Bedwells Heath OX1	22 B2
Beech Cres OX5	7 E5
Beech Croft Rd OX2	11 E1
Beech Rd, Botley OX2	18 A2
Beech Rd, Headington OX3	12 D5
Beech Rd, Wheatley OX33	15 F5
Beech Rd, Witney OX8	27 C1
Beechey Av OX3	12 A4
Beeching Way OX33	15 E4
Beef La OX1	4 D5
Begbroke Bsns & Science Pk OX5	6 B3
Begbroke Cres OX5	6 A2
Begbroke La OX5	6 A2
Belbroughton Rd OX2	11 F2
Belgrove Cl OX5	6 D3
Bell La OX33	15 F4
Bellenger Way OX5	6 D3
Belvedere Rd OX4	20 C3
Ben Cl OX5	7 E1
Benmead Rd OX5	6 D2
Bennett Cres OX4	21 E5
Benson Pl OX2	11 G3
Benson Rd OX3	21 E2
Bergamot Pl OX4	25 F4
Berkeley Rd OX1	22 B2
Bernard Cl OX5	6 C6
Bernwood Rd OX3	13 F3
Berry Cl OX4	25 G1
Berrymere Rd OX13	17 C6
Bertie Pl OX1	19 H5
Bertie Rd OX2	16 B5
Besselsleigh Rd OX13	17 A4
Betty La OX1	19 F5
Between Towns Rd OX4	20 D6
Bevington Rd OX2	11 F4
Bhandari Cl OX4	20 C4
Bicester Rd, Gosford OX5	7 F6
Bicester Rd, Kidlington OX5	7 E3
Bickerton Rd OX3	12 D6
Binsey La OX2	10 C3
Binswood Av OX3	13 F6
Birch Rd OX44	26 A2
Birchfield Cl OX4	25 F2
Biscoe Ct OX33	15 G4
Bishop Kirk Pl OX2	9 E6
Bishops Wood OX44	26 F1
Blackberry La OX4	25 H4
Blackbird Leys Rd OX4	25 E1
Blackfriars Rd OX1	4 C6
Blackhall Rd OX1	4 D1
Blackman Cl OX1	23 H1
Blacksmiths Mdw OX4	25 G3
Blackstock Cl OX3	21 F3
Blackthorn Cl OX3	13 E4
Bladon Cl OX2	8 D5
Blandford Av OX2	8 D4
Blandford Rd OX5	6 C1
Blankstone Cl OX8	27 B3
Blay Cl OX4	25 F2
Bleache Pl OX4	21 E5
Blenheim Cl OX2	9 E5
Blenheim Dr OX2	8 D5
Blenheim La OX33	15 E4
Blenheim Rd, Horspath OX33	14 B6
Blenheim Rd, Kidlington OX5	7 F3
Blenheim Way OX33	14 B6
Blewitt Ct*, Oxford Rd OX4	24 C2
Blomfield Pl OX2	4 B1
Blue Boar St OX1	5 E5
Bluebell Ct OX4	25 G3
Bobby Fryer Cl OX4	21 F6
Bodley Pl OX2	9 F4
Bodley Rd OX4	24 D1
Bonar Rd OX3	21 F1
Bonn Sq OX1	4 D4
Borrowmead Rd OX3	12 C3
Boswell Rd OX4	21 E6
Botley Rd OX2	4 A4
Boulter St OX4	20 A1
Boults Cl OX3	12 B3
Boults La OX3	12 A3
Boundary Brook Rd OX4	20 B4
Boundary Cl OX20	3 C2
Bourne Cl OX2	9 E4
Bowerman Cl OX5	6 D3
Bowness Av OX3	12 C4
Bracegirdle Rd OX3	21 F2
Bradlands OX3	12 A1
Bradley Cotts OX2	17 B1
Bradmore Rd OX2	11 F3
Brake Hill OX4	25 G3
Brambling Way OX4	25 E2
Brampton Rd OX3	13 F4
Bramwell Pl OX4	20 B3
Brandon Cl OX5	6 D3
Brasenose Dr OX5	7 E2
Brasenose Driftway OX4	21 F4
Brasenose La OX1	5 E4
Brewer St OX1	4 D5
Briar End OX5	3 D6
Briar Thicket OX20	3 C2
Briar Way OX4	25 G2
Brick Kiln La OX4	24 C5
Bridge St OX2	4 A4
Broad Cl, Kidlington OX5	6 D3
Broad Cl, Oxford OX2	16 D1
Broad Field Rd OX5	6 B4
Broad Oak OX3	21 F2
Broad St OX1	5 E3
Broad Walk OX1	5 F5
Broadfields OX4	25 E2
Broadhead Pl OX3	12 C3
Broadhurst Gdns OX4	24 B3
Brocklesby Rd OX4	24 B2
Brogden Cl OX2	18 B2
Brome Pl OX3	13 F4
Brook Hill OX20	3 B2
Brook St OX1	19 G2
Brook Vw OX4	25 H2
Brookfield Cres OX3	12 B3
Brooklime Walk OX4	25 F3
Brooks Taylor Ct OX1	4 D6
Brookside OX3	12 D6
Broughton Cl OX3	12 A3
Browns Cl OX2	16 C2
Browns La OX20	3 B2
Brumcombe La OX13	22 D4
Bryony Cl OX4	25 H2
Buckingham St OX1	19 G2
Buckland Ct OX5	7 F3
Buckler Pl OX4	24 B3
Buckler Rd OX2	9 F5
Budds Cl OX20	3 D1
Bulan Rd OX3	21 E2
Bullingdon Rd OX4	20 A3
Bullsmead OX13	22 C6
Bullstake Cl OX2	10 C6
Bulrush Rd OX4	25 G3
Bulwarks La OX1	4 D4
Burbush Rd OX4	21 F5
Burchester Av OX3	13 F4
Burdell Av OX3	13 H4
Burgan Cl OX4	21 E6
Burlington Cres OX3	13 H5
Burra Cl OX4	24 B5
Burrows Cl OX3	13 E5
Bursill Cl OX3	13 H5
Burton Pl OX4	21 F4
Bushey Cl OX2	16 D1
Bushey Leys Cl OX3	13 F3
Butler Cl, Horspath OX33	14 B6
Butler Cl, Oxford OX2	11 F3
Buttercup Sq OX4	25 G3
Butterworth Pl OX4	25 G2
Butterwyke Pl OX1	4 D6
Butts La OX3	12 A2
Butts Rd OX33	14 B6
Cadogan Pk OX20	3 C2
Calcot Cl OX3	21 F1
Calves Cl OX5	6 D3
Cambridge Ter OX1	4 D6
Campbell Cl OX20	3 C2
Campbell Rd OX4	20 B5
Campion Cl OX4	25 G3
Canal Pl OX2	4 B2
Canal Rd OX5	3 C4
Canal St OX2	4 A1
Canal Vw OX5	7 E4
Candy Way OX13	17 D6
Canning Cres OX1	19 H4
Cannons Fld OX2	12 A2
Canterbury Rd OX2	11 F3
Capel Cl OX2	9 E5
Cardigan St OX2	4 B1
Cardinal Cl OX4	24 C1
Cardwell Cres OX3	12 C6
Carey Cl OX2	8 D4
Carlton Rd OX2	9 E4
Caroline Ct OX20	3 B2
Caroline St OX4	20 A1
Carpenter Cl OX4	24 D3
Carter Cl OX3	13 G6
Cassington Rd, Kidlington OX5	6 A6
Cassington Rd, Witney OX8	27 D2
Castle Mews OX1	4 B4
Castle St OX1	4 D5
Catherine St OX4	20 B3
Catte St OX1	5 F3
Catwell Cl OX4	20 D4
Cave St OX4	20 A1
Cavell Rd OX4	20 B5
Cavendish Dr OX3	12 A3
Cavendish Rd OX2	9 E4
Cecil Sharp Pl OX3	13 E6
Cedar Ct OX4	20 D5
Cedar Rd OX2	18 A2
Cedar Vw OX44	26 A2
Celandine Pl OX4	25 G3
Centaury Pl OX3	25 H2
Centre Rise OX33	14 C6
Centremead OX2	18 D1
Century Row*, Middle Way OX2	9 E6
Chadlington Rd OX2	11 G2
Chaffinch Walk OX4	25 G3
Chain Alley OX1	4 C3
Chalfont Rd OX2	11 E2
Chamberlain Pl OX5	6 C2
Champion Way OX4	24 D2
Chapel La OX4	24 C2
Chapel St OX4	20 B2
Chapel Way OX2	10 B6
Charlbury Cl OX5	6 C1
Charlbury Rd OX2	11 F1
Charles St OX4	20 B4
Chatham Rd OX1	19 H4
Chaucers La OX20	3 A2
Chawley La OX2	16 B4
Cheltenham Rd OX8	27 A1
Cheney La OX3	20 B1
Chequers Pl OX3	13 F5
Cherry Cl, Blackbird Leys OX4	25 G3
Cherry Cl, Kidlington OX5	7 E4
Cherwell Av OX5	7 F2
Cherwell Bsns Centre OX5	13 D6
Cherwell Dr OX3	12 A3
Cherwell St OX4	20 A1
Chester St OX4	20 A4
Chestnut Av OX3	13 E4
Chestnut Rd OX2	18 A2
Chilbridge Rd OX8	27 A3
Chillingworth Cres OX3	21 F2
Chilswell La OX1	18 C6
Chilswell Path OX1	18 C6
Chilswell Rd OX1	19 G2
Chiltern Bsns Centre OX4	21 F6
Cholesbury Grange OX3	12 B4
Cholsey Cl OX4	21 E6
Chorefields OX5	6 D2
Choswell Spring OX4	25 F3
Church Cl, Cuddesdon OX44	26 F2
Church Cl, Oxford OX1	19 F4
Church Cowley Rd OX4	20 C6
Church Hill Rd OX4	20 C6
Church La, Oxford OX3	12 A1
Church La, Wolvercote OX2	8 C5
Church La, Yarnton OX5	6 B6
Church Rd, Horspath OX33	14 B6
Church Rd, Sandford-on-Thame OX4	24 B5
Church Rd, Wheatley OX33	15 F4
Church St, Kidlington OX5	7 E1
Church St, Witney OX8	27 C2
Church Walk OX2	11 F3
Church Way, Botley OX2	10 A6
Church Way, Iffley OX4	20 A6
Churchill Cl OX20	3 C1
Churchill Dr OX3	21 E1
Churchill Gate OX20	3 C3
Churchill Pl OX2	8 C5
Churchill Rd OX5	7 E3
Cinnaminta Rd OX3	21 F2
Circus St OX4	20 A2
Clarendon Centre OX1	4 D4
Clarks Row OX1	5 E6
Claymond Rd OX3	13 G4
Clays Cl OX3	12 B3
Cleavers Sq OX4	25 F3
Clematis Pl OX4	25 G2
Cleveland Cl OX5	7 F4
Cleveland Dr OX4	20 D5
Clifford Pl OX2	8 B5
Clinton Cl OX4	24 A2
Clive Rd OX4	20 C5
Clover Cl OX2	16 D4
Clover Pl, Oxford OX4	25 G3
Clover Pl, Witney OX8	27 B2
Cobden Cres OX1	19 G2
Cockpit Cl OX20	3 B2
Colemans Hill OX3	13 F5
Coleridge Cl OX4	21 E6
Colgrove Down OX2	16 C4
Collcutt Cl OX33	14 B6
College Cl OX33	15 G4
College La OX4	24 C2
College Way OX33	14 A6
Colley Wood OX1	23 G1
Collins St OX4	20 B2
Collinwood Cl OX3	13 G5
Collinwood Rd OX3	13 G5
Colterne Cl OX3	12 B4
Coltsfoot Sq OX4	25 G3
Columbine Gdns OX4	25 H3
Colwell Dr OX3	13 H4
Combe Rd OX2	4 A1
Combewell OX44	26 A2
Comfrey Rd OX4	25 G1
Compass Cl OX4	20 D6
Complins Cl OX2	11 E1
Conduit La OX8	27 B2
Conifer Cl OX4	18 A1
Coniston Av OX3	12 B4
Coolidge Cl OX3	21 E1
Coombe Cl OX3	15 F5
Cooper Pl OX3	13 G5
Coopers Cl OX3	15 E5
Cope Cl OX2	18 A1
Coppock Cl OX3	13 F5
Copse La OX3	12 B4
Copthorne Rd OX5	7 E4
Cordrey Grn OX4	20 B6
Coriander Way OX4	25 G3
Cornmarket St OX1	4 D3
Cornwallis Cl OX4	20 B5
Cornwallis Rd OX4	20 B5
Corruna Cres OX4	21 F4
Cosin Cl OX4	20 B2
Costar Cl OX4	25 E2
Cots Grn OX5	6 D1
Cotswold Cres OX3	12 A3
Cotswold Rd OX2	16 D3
Cottesmore Rd OX4	24 B2
Cotton Grass Cl OX4	25 F3
County Trading Est OX4	25 G1
Coupland Rd OX13	17 C
Court Cl OX5	6 D
Court Farm Rd OX4	24 A
Court Place Gdns OX4	24 A
Courtland Rd OX3	20 B
Coverley Rd OX3	21 E
Cow La OX1	24 A
Cowley Pl OX4	5 H
Cowley Rd, Littlemore OX4	24 C
Cowley Rd, Oxford OX4	5 H
Coxs Ground OX2	10 D
Crabtree Rd OX2	18 B
Cranbrook Dr OX1	23 H
Cranesbill Way OX4	25 F
Cranham St OX2	4 A
Cranham Ter OX2	4 B
Cranley Rd OX3	13 G
Cranmer Rd OX4	21 F
Cranston Cl OX4	24 C
Craufurd Rd OX4	21 F
Crecy Walk OX20	3 C
Cres Cl OX4	21 E
Crescent Rd OX4	20 D
Cress Hill Pl OX3	13 G
Crick Rd OX2	11 G
Cricket Rd OX4	20 B
Cripley Pl OX2	4 A
Cripley Rd OX2	4 A
Croft Av OX5	7 E
Croft Cl OX3	12 A
Croft Rd OX3	12 A
Cromwell Cl OX3	12 A
Cromwell St OX1	5 E
Cromwell Way OX5	7 F
Cross St OX4	20 A
Crotch Cres OX3	12 B
Crowberry Rd OX4	25 G
Crowell Rd OX4	20 D
Crown Rd, Kidlington OX5	6 D
Crown Rd, Wheatley OX33	15 G
Crown St OX4	20 A
Croxford Gdns OX5	7 E
Crozier Cl OX2	18 B
Cuckoo La, Oxford OX4	12 B
Cuckoo La, Witney OX8	27 A
Cuddesdon Rd OX33	14 B
Cuddesdon Way OX4	25 F
Cullum Ho OX33	15 G
Cullum Rd OX33	15 G
Cumberland Rd OX4	20 C
Cumberlege Cl OX3	12 A
Cummings Cl OX3	13 F
Cumnor Hill OX2	16 B
Cumnor Hill By-Pass OX2	16 B
Cumnor Rd OX1	17 B
Cumnor Rise Rd OX2	18 A
Cunliffe Cl OX2	11 F
Curtis Rd OX5	6 D
Cyprus Ter OX2	8 D
Dale Cl OX1	4 C
Dale Pl OX5	7 E
Danvers Rd OX4	24 B
Dark La OX13	22 C
Dashwood Av OX5	6 B
Dashwood Rd OX4	24 B
Daubeny Rd OX4	20 A
Davenant Rd OX2	8 D
David Nicholls Cl OX4	24 C
David Walter Cl OX2	9 E
Dawson Pl OX2	4 A
Dawson St OX4	20 A
Dead Mans Walk OX1	5 F
Deanfield Rd OX2	16 D
Deans Court Rd OX2	16 D
Deaufort Cl OX5	7 E
Deer Walk OX4	25 G
Delamare Way OX2	16 D
Delbush Av OX3	13 H
Dene Rd OX3	21 E
Denmans La OX2	16 A
Denmark St OX4	20 A
Denton Cl OX2	16 C
Denton Hill OX44	26 F

enton La OX44 26 B3
ents Cl OX3 12 B3
erwent Av OX3 12 B4
esborough Cres
)X4 24 B1
esmesne Furze OX3 20 D1
evereux Pl OX4 24 C1
evine Cl OX4 20 B4
iamond Pl OX2 11 F1
ivinity Rd OX4 20 B3
odgson Rd OX4 20 D6
on Boscoe Cl OX4 21 E4
on Stuart Pl OX4 20 C3
onnington Bridge Rd
)X1 19 H4
ora Carr Cl OX3 12 C3
orchester Cl OX3 21 F1
oris Field Cl OX3 12 B4
ove End OX8 27 C1
ove House Cl OX2 8 C5
ovehouse Cl OX8 27 C1
ownside End OX3 13 H5
ownside Rd OX3 13 G6
oyley Rd OX2 19 E1
rewitt Ct OX2 8 B5
rove Acre Rd OX4 20 B3
ruce Way OX4 25 G1
udgeon Dr OX4 24 C2
udley Ct OX2 9 E6
udley Gdns*,
Cave St OX4 20 A1
uke St OX2 10 D6
ukes Rd OX5 7 E2
uncan Cl OX8 27 B1
unnock Way OX4 25 F3
unstan Rd OX3 12 D4
ynham Pl OX3 21 E1

arl St OX2 10 C6
ast Av OX4 20 B2
ast Field Ct OX3 21 F3
ast St OX2 4 A4
astchurch OX4 24 A1
astern Av OX4 24 C1
astern By-Pass OX3 13 G5
astern By-Pass Rd
OX4 24 B2
den Dr OX3 12 C3
dgecombe Rd OX3 13 F4
dgeway Rd OX3 12 A5
dinburgh Dr OX5 7 F3
dith Rd OX1 19 G3
dmund Halley Rd
OX4 24 D4
dmund Rd OX4 20 D5
dward Abraham Rd
OX1 5 F1
dward Rd OX1 23 H2
dwin Ct OX2 10 D6
gerton Rd OX4 20 B6
ighth Av OX3 21 G2
lder Way OX4 25 G3
leanor Cl OX4 20 C6
lectric Av OX2 18 D1
llesmere Rd OX4 20 B6
lm Cl OX33 15 G5
lm Dr OX44 26 A2
lm Gro OX5 7 E5
lm Tree Cl OX4 24 C1
lor Dr OX3 12 B3
lms Par OX2 10 A6
lms Rd OX2 10 A6
lmthorpe Rd OX2 8 B4
lsfield Rd OX3 12 A2
lsfield Way OX3 9 E4
lton Cres OX33 15 G5
mperor Gdns OX4 25 F3
rica Cl OX4 25 G2
ssex St OX4 20 B3
thelred Ct OX3 12 D4
vans Cl OX8 27 C2
vans Ct OX5 7 F3
vans La OX5 7 F3
velyn Cl OX2 16 D2
venlode Cres OX5 3 B6
verard Cl OX3 21 E1
wert Pl OX2 11 F1
win Cl OX5 12 B3
xeter Rd OX5 7 E2
ynsham Rd OX2 16 A1
yot Pl OX4 20 A3

Faber Cl OX4 24 D3
Fair Vw OX3 21 E3
Fairacres Rd OX4 20 A4
Fairfax Gate OX33 15 G4
Fairfax Rd,
Kidlington OX5 7 F5
Fairfax Rd,
Oxford OX4 21 F4
Fairlawn End OX2 8 D4
Fairlie Rd OX4 24 C1
Falcon Cl OX4 25 E2
Falstaff Rd OX8 27 B2
Fane Rd OX3 12 A3
Fanshawe Pl OX4 21 F5
Faringdon Rd OX13 17 A4
Farm Cl,
Kidlington OX5 7 E1
Farm Cl, Oxford OX4 25 G3
Farm Close La OX33 15 F5
Farm Close Rd OX33 15 F5
Farm End OX20 3 A1
Farmer Pl OX3 12 A4
Farndon Rd OX2 11 E3
Faulkner St OX1 4 D6
Feildon Gro OX3 12 B5
Fern Hill Rd OX4 21 E5
Fernhill Cl OX5 6 D3
Fernhill Rd OX5 6 A2
Ferry Hinksey Rd
OX2 10 D6
Ferry La OX3 12 A5
Ferry Mills OX2 18 D1
Ferry Pool Rd OX2 11 F1
Ferry Rd OX3 12 A5
Fettiplace Rd OX3 13 F3
Field Av OX4 25 G2
Field Cl,
Kidlington OX5 7 E2
Field Cl, Yarnton OX5 6 B5
Field House Dr OX2 9 E5
Field La OX44 26 F2
Fieldfare Rd OX4 25 F4
Fiennes Rd OX4 24 C1
Finch Cl OX4 20 D1
Finmore Rd OX2 18 B1
Firs Mdw OX4 25 F4
First Av OX3 21 G3
First Turn OX2 8 C5
Fitzherbert Cl OX4 20 A6
Five Mile Dr OX3 8 D4
Flatford Pl OX4 6 C1
Flaxfield Rd OX4 25 G3
Flemings Rd OX20 3 D2
Fletcher Cl OX5 6 B5
Fletcher Rd OX4 21 F4
Flexney Pl OX3 21 E1
Florence Cl OX5 7 E3
Florence Park Rd
OX4 20 C6
Florey Rd OX1 5 F1
Floyds Row OX1 5 E6
Fogwell Rd OX2 16 C1
Follets Cl OX5 6 B6
Fords Cl OX33 14 B6
Forest Rd OX3 13 G5
Forest Side OX1 23 G1
Forget-Me-Not Way
OX4 25 F3
Forster Rd OX2 16 A6
Fortnam Cl OX3 12 C5
Fourth Av OX3 21 G2
Fox Cl OX4 20 C6
Fox Cres OX1 19 H4
Fox Furlong OX4 24 B3
Fox La OX1,13 22 A5
Foxcombe Dr OX1 22 C3
Foxcombe La OX1 22 D2
Foxcombe Rd OX1 22 C3
Foxdown Cl OX5 7 E2
Foxglove Rd OX5 6 B2
Foxton Cl OX3 8 D4
Foxwell Dr OX3 12 C3
Franklin Cl OX5 7 E1
Franklin Rd OX4 12 C5
Frederick Rd OX4 21 E6
Freeborn Cl OX5 7 E1
Freelands Rd OX4 20 A5
Frenchay Rd OX2 11 E2
Frewin Ct OX1 4 D4
Friars Entry OX1 4 D3
Friars Wharf OX1 4 D6
Fridays La OX33 15 G4
Frieze Way OX5 7 F6

Frogwelldown La
OX5 6 A6
Fruitlands OX8 27 A1
Frys Hill OX4 25 F4
Furlong Cl OX4 25 E2
Fyfield Rd OX2 11 G3

Gaisford Rd OX4 20 D6
Galpin Cl OX4 20 B3
Gardiner Cl OX33 15 F4
Gardiner St OX3 13 E6
Garford Rd OX2 11 G2
Garsington Rd OX4 21 E5
Gateley OX33 14 C6
Gathorne Rd OX3 13 E6
Gentian Rd OX4 25 G3
George Moore Cl
OX4 20 B4
George St OX1 4 C3
George St Mews OX1 4 C4
Gerard Pl OX4 20 D5
Gibbs Cres OX2 4 B6
Gidley Way OX33 14 B6
Giles Cl OX4 24 D2
Giles St OX4 24 D2
Gillians Way OX4 20 C4
Gipsy La OX3 12 C6
Girdlestone Cl OX3 21 E1
Girdlestone Rd OX3 21 E1
Gladstone Ct*,
Gladstone Rd OX4 13 F5
Gladstone Rd OX3 13 F5
Glanville Rd OX4 20 C4
Glebe Rd OX2 16 A5
Glebe St OX4 20 A2
Glebelands OX3 21 E2
Gloucester Grn OX1 4 C3
Gloucester La OX1 4 C3
Gloucester Pl OX1 4 D3
Gloucester St OX1 4 D3
Glovers Cl OX20 3 C2
Glyme Cl OX20 3 B1
Glyme Vw OX20 3 A1
Godstow Rd OX2 8 A6
Golden Cross OX1 5 E4
Golden Rd OX4 20 B4
Goodson Walk OX3 12 A5
Goose Green Cl OX4 8 C4
Gordon Cl OX3 12 A3
Gordon St OX1 19 G3
Gorse Leas OX3 12 C3
Gosford Cl OX5 7 F5
Goslyn Cl OX3 21 E1
Gouldland Gdns OX3 12 C3
Grandpont Pl OX1 19 F1
Grange Ct OX2 16 D1
Grange Mill Ct OX8 27 B2
Grange Rd OX4 24 D2
Grants Mews OX4 20 A2
Granville Ct OX3 20 B1
Gravel Pits La OX5 6 B5
Grays Rd OX3 12 C6
Great Clarendon St
OX2 4 B2
Great Close Rd OX5 6 B6
Great Mead OX1 4 B3
Grebe Cl OX4 25 F4
Green Hill OX4 25 H2
Green La,
Abingdon OX13 22 D4
Green La,
Oxford OX4 16 C2
Green La,
Woodstock OX20 3 B1
Green Pl OX1 19 G3
Green Rd,
Kidlington OX5 7 F5
Green Rd,
Oxford OX3 13 G5
Green Ridges OX3 13 H4
Green St OX4 20 B3
Greenfinch Cl OX4 25 G3
Greens Rd OX8 27 B1
Grenoble Rd OX4 25 E3
Greystones Ct OX5 6 D2
Grosvenor Rd OX3 18 C3
Grove St OX3 9 E6
Grovelands OX5 6 D2
Grovelands Rd OX3 13 H6
Grundy Cres OX1 23 H3
Grunsell Cl OX3 12 D3
Guelder Rd OX4 25 F4
Gurden Pl OX3 13 F4

Gurl Cl OX3 13 F4
Gwyneth Rd OX4 24 B2

Hadow Rd OX3 12 B4
Haldane Rd OX4 25 F2
Halliday Hill OX3 12 C3
Halls Cl OX2 16 D4
Hamels La OX1 22 D2
Hamilton Rd OX2 9 F6
Hampden Dr OX5 7 F5
Hampden Rd OX4 20 D6
Hanborough Cl OX8 27 C1
Hanborough Rd OX8 27 C1
Handlo Pl OX3 13 G4
Harberton Mead OX3 12 B5
Harbord Rd OX2 9 E3
Harcourt Hill OX2 18 B3
Harcourt Ter OX3 12 C6
Hardings Cl OX4 24 D1
Hardwick Av OX5 7 E3
Harebell Rd OX4 25 G2
Harefields OX3 9 E4
Harley Rd OX4 10 D6
Harlow Way OX3 12 A1
Harold White Cl OX3 13 G6
Harolde Cl OX3 13 F4
Harpes Rd OX2 9 F5
Harpsichord Pl OX4 20 A1
Harrisons La OX20 3 B2
Harrow Rd OX4 25 G1
Hart St OX2 4 B1
Hartley Russell Cl
OX4 20 B5
Harts Cl OX5 6 D3
Haslemere Gdns OX2 9 E3
Hastoe Grange OX3 12 C4
Hathaways OX33 15 F4
Havelock Rd OX4 20 D5
Hawkins St OX4 20 B3
Hawkins Way OX13 17 D6
Hawksmoor Rd OX2 9 E4
Hawkswell Gdns OX2 9 F6
Hawthorn Av OX3 13 E5
Hawthorn Cl OX2 18 B1
Hawthorn Rd OX2 27 C2
Hawthorn Way OX5 7 E4
Hayes Cl OX3 12 A5
Hayfield Rd OX2 11 E2
Haynes Rd OX3 12 A3
Hayward Rd OX2 9 E3
Hazel Cres OX5 7 E5
Hazel End OX44 26 A2
Hazel Rd OX2 10 A6
Hazel Walk OX5 7 E5
Headington Hill OX3 20 C1
Headington Rd OX3 20 B1
Headley Way OX3 12 B4
Heath Cl OX3 21 E2
Heather Pl OX3 12 A5
Heatley Rd OX4 24 C4
Hedge End OX20 3 C2
Hedges Cl OX3 13 F5
Helen Rd OX2 10 D6
Helleborine Cl OX4 25 G3
Helwys Pl OX5 6 D1
Hendred Ho OX4 20 C4
Hendred St OX4 20 C5
Hengrove Cl OX3 13 E4
Henley Av OX4 20 B5
Henley Rd OX4 24 C4
Henley St OX4 20 A3
Henry Taunt Cl OX3 13 F3
Hensington Cl OX20 3 D1
Hensington Rd OX20 3 B2
Henwood Dr OX1 17 C3
Herbert Cl OX4 20 C3
Hernes Cl OX2 9 F5
Hernes Cres OX2 9 E5
Heron Pl OX2 9 F5
Herschel Cres OX4 24 D1
Hertford St OX4 20 B3
Heycroft OX8 27 C3
Heyford Hill La OX4 24 A2
Heyford Mead OX5 6 D2
Hids Copse Rd OX2 16 D1
High Cross Way OX3 13 F3
High St,
Cuddesdon OX44 26 F2
High St,
Cumnor OX2 16 A5
High St,
Eynsham OX8 27 C2

High St,
Kidlington OX5 6 D2
High St, Oxford OX1 5 E4
High St,
Wheatley OX33 15 F4
High St,
Woodstock OX20 3 B2
Highfield Av OX3 20 D1
Hill Rise OX33 14 C6
Hill Top Rd OX4 21 E5
Hill View La OX1 17 C4
Hill View Rd OX3 10 D6
Hill Vw OX3 21 E3
Hillary Way OX33 15 G5
Hillsborough Cl OX4 24 C1
Hillsborough Rd OX4 24 C1
Hillside OX2 16 C4
Hinksey Hill OX1 23 E1
Hinshelwood Rd OX1 5 F1
Hobby Cl OX4 25 G4
Hobson Rd OX2 9 E6
Hockmore St OX4 20 B6
Hodges Ct OX1 19 G2
Holland Pl OX3 21 F2
Holley Cres OX3 13 F5
Hollow Way OX4 21 E5
Holloway Rd OX33 15 F4
Holly Cl OX5 7 E4
Hollybush Row OX1 4 B4
Holt Weer Cl OX2 9 F4
Holyoake Rd OX3 13 E5
Holywell Bsns Centre
OX2 18 D1
Holywell St OX1 5 F3
Home Cl,
Abingdon OX13 17 D6
Home Cl,
Kidlington OX5 7 E2
Home Cl,
Wolvercote OX2 8 B4
Homestall Cl OX2 16 D1
Honeysuckle Gro
OX4 25 H2
Honor Cl OX5 7 E3
Hornbeam Dr OX4 25 H2
Horseman Cl OX3 12 B3
Horspath Driftway
OX3 21 F3
Horspath Rd OX4 21 E4
Horspath Rd Ind Est
OX4 21 G4
Horwood Cl OX3 12 D6
Hosker Cl OX3 13 H4
Howard St OX4 20 B4
Howe Cl OX33 15 F5
Hubble Cl OX3 13 F3
Hugh Allen Cres OX3 12 A5
Humfrey Rd OX3 13 G4
Hundred Acre Cl OX3 21 F3
Hunsdon Rd OX4 20 B6
Hunter Cl OX4 21 F4
Hurst La OX2 16 C4
Hurst Rise Rd OX2 18 A1
Hurst St OX4 20 A2
Hutchcomb Rd OX2 18 A1
Hutchcombe Farm Cl
OX2 18 A2
Huxley Cl OX3 17 D6
Hyacinth Walk OX4 25 F4
Hyde Pl OX2 9 E6
Hythe Bridge St OX1 4 B4

Iffley Rd OX4 5 H5
Iffley Turn OX4 20 B5
Ilsley Rd OX3 13 F4
Ingle Cl OX3 12 C4
Inott Furze OX3 21 E3
Islip Pl OX2 9 F5
Islip Rd OX2 9 F5
Ivy La OX3 12 D4

Jack Argent Pl OX4 25 G3
Jack Straws La OX3 12 B5
Jackdaw La OX4 20 A3
Jackies La OX33 15 G5
Jackson Cole Ho*,
StThomas St OX1 4 C4
Jackson Rd,
Kennington OX1 23 H1
Jackson Rd,
Oxford OX2 9 F4
James St OX4 20 A3
James Wolf Rd OX4 21 F3

Janaway Pl OX4	24 B3
Jarn Way OX1	22 B2
Jasmine Cl OX4	25 G2
Jericho St OX2	4 B1
Jersey Rd OX4	24 B1
Jessops Cl OX3	12 B3
Jeune St OX4	20 A2
Joan Lawrence Pl OX3	21 F1
Joe Whites La OX2	8 B4
John Allen Way OX4	20 D6
John Buchan Rd OX3	12 C3
John Garne Way OX3	12 B6
John Kallie Ct OX4	20 C4
John Lopes Rd OX8	27 C2
John Piers La OX1	14 C4
John Smith Dr OX4	21 E6
John Snow Pl OX3	13 F5
John Towle Cl OX1	19 G4
Jordan Hill OX2	9 E3
Jourdain Rd OX4	25 G1
Jowett Walk OX1	5 F3
Judges Cl OX5	6 D2
Junction Rd OX4	21 E5
Juniper Dr OX4	25 G2
Juxon St OX2	4 A1
Kames Cl OX4	20 C5
Keble Rd OX1	4 D1
Keene Cl OX4	24 C4
Kelburne Rd OX4	20 C6
Kelham Hall Dr OX33	15 F5
Kellys Rd OX33	14 D5
Kempson Cres OX4	24 C2
Kendall Cres OX2	9 F4
Kenilworth Av OX4	20 C3
Kenilworth Ct OX4	20 C3
Kenilworth Rd OX2	16 A6
Kennedy Cl OX4	21 F4
Kennett Rd OX3	13 E5
Kennington Rd, Abingdon OX14	24 A6
Kennington Rd, Kennington OX1	19 G5
Kent Cl OX4	25 F1
Kenville Rd OX1	23 H1
Kersington Cres OX4	25 E1
Kerwood Cl OX20	3 C1
Kestrel Cres OX4	25 E2
Keydale Rd OX33	14 D5
Kidlington Bsns Centre OX5	3 D6
Kiln Cl OX4	24 D4
Kiln La, Garsington OX44	26 A3
Kiln La, Headington OX3	13 G6
Kiln La, Wheatley OX33	15 F4
Kimber Cl OX33	15 F5
Kineton Rd OX1	19 G2
King Edward St OX1	5 F4
King St OX2	4 B1
King William Ho*, St Thomas St OX1	4 C4
Kingfisher Grn OX4	25 G3
Kings Cross Rd OX2	9 F5
Kings Mdw Ind Est OX2	18 D1
Kings Mill La OX3	12 A6
Kings Way Dr OX5	7 F3
Kingston Cl OX2	11 E4
Kingston Rd OX2	11 E3
Kirby Pl OX4	21 E5
Kirk Cl, Kennington OX1	23 H3
Kirk Cl, Oxford OX2	8 D4
Knights Rd OX4	25 E3
Knolles Rd OX4	20 D6
Kybald St OX1	5 F4
Laburnum Cres OX5	7 E4
Laburnum Rd OX2	18 B2
Ladder Hill OX33	15 F6
Ladenham Rd OX4	25 F1
Lake St OX1	19 G3
Lakefield Rd OX4	24 C3
Lakeside OX2	8 D3
Lakesmere Cl OX5	3 D6
Lamborough Hill OX13	17 C5
Lambourn Rd OX4	24 B1
Lambs Cl OX5	7 E1
Lampton Cl OX4	21 F4
Lane Cl OX5	6 C3
Langford Bsns Pk OX5	3 C6
Langford La OX5	3 A6
Langford Locks OX5	3 D6
Langley Cl OX3	13 E6
Lanham Way OX4	24 C2
Lansdowne Rd OX13	17 C6
Larch Cl OX2	18 B1
Larch End OX44	26 A2
Larkfields OX3	13 F6
Larkins La OX3	13 E4
Lashford La OX13	17 B5
Lathbury Rd OX2	11 F2
Latimer Grange OX3	12 D6
Latimer Rd OX3	12 D6
Laurel Farm Cl OX3	12 D4
Lawrence Rd OX4	20 D5
Le Gros Clark Pl OX1	5 F1
Leafield Rd OX4	21 E4
Leckford Pl OX2	11 E4
Leckford Rd OX2	11 E4
Lee Cl OX5	6 D1
Leiden Rd OX3	21 F2
Leigh Croft OX13	17 C5
Lenthall Rd OX4	24 B1
Leon Cl OX4	20 B3
Leopold St OX4	20 B3
Lewell Av OX3	12 A4
Lewin Cl OX4	20 D6
Lewis Cl OX3	13 G6
Leys Pl OX4	20 B3
Leyshon Rd OX33	15 G5
Liddell Rd OX4	20 D6
Liddiard Cl OX1	23 H3
Lime Rd OX2	18 B2
Lime Walk OX3	12 D6
Lincoln Rd OX1	19 G4
Lincombe La OX1	22 C3
Lincraft Cl OX5	7 E4
Links Rd OX1	23 H4
Linkside Av OX2	8 D3
Linnet Cl OX4	25 E2
Linton Rd OX2	11 F2
Litford Cl OX4	24 C2
Little Acreage OX3	12 B2
Little Blenheim OX5	6 A6
Little Brewery St OX4	20 A1
Little Bury OX4	25 H2
Little Clarendon St OX1	4 C1
Littlegate St OX1	4 D6
Littlehay Rd OX4	20 C5
Littlemead Bsns Pk OX2	18 D1
Littlemore Rd OX4	20 D6
Littleworth Bsns Centre OX33	15 F4
Littleworth Rd OX33	14 D6
Livingstone Cl OX5	6 B4
Lobelia Rd OX4	25 G3
Lock Cres OX5	7 E5
Lockheart Cres OX4	25 E1
Lodge Cl OX3	12 A1
Logic La OX1	5 F4
Lombard St OX8	27 C2
London Ct OX3	12 D6
London Pl OX4	20 A1
London Rd, Oxford OX3	12 D6
London Rd, Wheatley OX33	15 F4
Long Cl, Botley OX2	16 D1
Long Cl, Headington OX3	21 F2
Long Ford Cl OX1	19 F2
Long Grnd OX4	25 F3
Long La OX4	24 D1
Longlands Rd OX4	25 F1
Longwall OX4	24 C2
Longwall St OX1	5 G3
Longworth Rd OX2	11 E4
Lonsdale Rd OX2	9 F6
Lovelace Dr OX5	7 F3
Lovelace Rd OX2	9 E4
Lovelace Sq OX2	9 E3
Lower Fisher Row OX1	4 C4
Lucas Pl OX1	20 A6
Lucerne Rd OX2	9 F5
Lucy Faithful Ho*, Faulkner St OX1	4 D6
Luther Ct OX1	5 E6
Luther St OX1	5 E6
Lydia Cl OX3	13 G4
Lye Valley OX3	21 E2
Lyndworth Cl OX3	13 F4
Lyndworth Mews OX3	13 F5
Lyne Rd OX5	6 C2
Lynn Cl OX3	12 B5
Lytton Rd OX4	20 C5
Magdalen Rd OX4	20 A4
Magdalen St OX1	4 D3
Magdalen St East OX1	4 D3
Magnolia Cl OX5	7 E4
Magpie La OX1	5 F4
Maidcroft Rd OX4	20 D5
Main Av OX4	24 D4
Malford Rd OX3	13 G4
Mallard Cl OX4	25 E2
Maltfield Rd OX3	12 C3
Mandelbrote Dr OX4	24 C3
Manor Dr OX33	14 B6
Manor Farm Rd OX33	14 A6
Manor Gro OX1	24 A5
Manor Pl OX1	5 H2
Manor Rd, Abingdon OX13	17 C5
Manor Rd, Oxford OX1	5 G2
Manor Rd, South Hinksey OX1	19 F4
Manor Rd, Woodstock OX20	3 A1
Manor Way OX5	7 E1
Mansfield Rd OX1	5 F1
Manzil Way OX4	20 B2
Maple Av OX5	7 E4
Maple Cl OX2	18 B1
Maple Cl OX5	7 E4
Margaret Rd OX3	13 E6
Marigold Cl OX4	25 G3
Marjoram Cl OX4	25 H3
Mark Rd OX3	13 F6
Market Pl OX20	3 B2
Market St, Oxford OX1	5 E4
Market St, Woodstock OX20	3 B2
Marlborough Av OX5	6 D1
Marlborough Cl, Kidlington OX5	6 D1
Marlborough Cl, Oxford OX4	24 C2
Marlborough Cl, Witney OX8	27 B1
Marlborough Cres OX20	3 B1
Marlborough Ct OX2	10 D6
Marlborough Pl OX8	27 B1
Marlborough Rd OX1	19 F1
Marriott Cl OX2	9 E4
Marsh Cl OX5	6 C6
Marsh La OX3	12 B3
Marsh Rd OX4	20 D4
Marshall Rd OX4	21 E4
Marston Ferry Rd OX2	11 F1
Marston Rd OX3	20 A1
Marston St OX4	20 A2
Martin Ct OX2	9 E6
Mascall Av OX3	21 F3
Masons Rd OX3	21 F1
Massey Cl OX3	21 E1
Mather Rd OX3	13 G4
Mathews Way OX13	17 D6
Mattock Cl OX3	13 E6
Mavor Cl OX20	3 A1
Mayfair Rd OX4	24 C1
Mayfield Rd OX2	9 F6
Mead La OX8	27 D2
Mead Way OX5	6 D1
Meaden Hill OX3	12 C3
Meadow La OX4	20 A3
Meadow Prospect OX2	8 B5
Meadow View Rd OX1	24 A4
Meadow Vw OX5	7 E1
Meadow Walk OX20	3 C2
Meadow Way OX5	6 B5
Mercury Rd OX4	25 G3
Mere Rd OX2	8 C4
Merewood Av OX3	13 H4
Merlin Rd OX4	25 F2
Merrivale Sq OX2	11 E3
Merton Cl OX8	27 B2
Merton Ct OX2	11 E3
Merton Gro OX1	5 F5
Merton St OX1	5 F5
Merton Way OX5	6 B6
Meyseys Cl OX3	21 F3
Middle Way OX2	9 E5
Mika Pl OX2	16 D2
Mileway Gdns OX3	20 D1
Mill End OX5	7 F2
Mill La, Iffley OX4	20 A6
Mill La, Marston OX3	9 H5
Mill Rd OX2	8 B5
Mill St, Kidlington OX5	7 E1
Mill St, Oxford OX2	4 A4
Mill St, Witney OX8	27 C2
Mill Street Mews OX8	27 C2
Millbank OX2	4 A5
Miller Rd OX33	15 H5
Millers Acre OX2	9 F3
Millham Way OX3	12 B5
Millmoor Cres OX8	27 C1
Millstream Ct OX2	8 B5
Millway Cl OX2	8 C5
Milne Pl OX3	12 D3
Milton Rd OX4	20 C4
Minchery Rd OX4	24 D3
Minns Bsns Pk OX2	10 B6
Minster Rd OX4	20 C2
Mistletoe Grn OX4	25 F4
Moberly Cl OX4	20 A2
Mole Pl OX4	25 G3
Monks Cl OX4	25 E2
Monmouth Rd OX1	19 G4
Montagu Rd OX2	18 A1
Moody Rd OX3	12 B5
Moorbank OX4	25 F2
Moorhen Walk OX4	25 F3
Moreton Rd OX2	11 F1
Morland Cl OX33	15 F4
Morrell Av OX4	20 A1
Morrell Cl OX5	6 D3
Morrell Cres OX4	24 C3
Morris Cres OX4	20 C4
Mortimer Dr OX3	12 A4
Mortimer Rd OX4	24 A1
Morton Av OX5	7 E3
Morton Cl OX5	7 E3
Mount Pl OX2	4 A1
Mount St OX2	4 A1
Mulberry Cl OX3	9 E5
Mulberry Dr OX33	15 G5
Mulcaster Av OX5	7 E2
Murray Cl OX2	11 F2
Museum Rd OX1	5 E2
Napier Rd OX4	21 E6
Nash Ct OX4	21 E6
Nelson St OX2	4 B2
Nether Durford Cl OX3	21 G3
Netherwoods Rd OX3	13 G6
Nettlebed Mead OX4	24 D3
New College La OX1	5 F3
New Cross Rd OX3	13 F5
New High St OX3	12 D6
New Inn Hall St OX1	4 D4
New Rd, Oxford OX1	4 C4
New Rd, Woodstock OX20	3 C2
New St OX4	20 A1
Newland Cl OX8	27 C2
Newland St OX8	27 C2
Newlin Cl OX4	24 B1
Newman Ct*, Cave St OX4	20 A1
Newman Rd OX4	24 C1
Newport Cl OX5	6 D3
Newton Rd OX1	19 G2
Nicholas Av OX3	12 A4
Nicholson Rd OX3	12 A5
Nightingale Av OX4	25 G3
Ninth Av OX3	21 G3
Nixon Rd OX4	20 B5
Nobles Cl OX2	16
Nobles La OX2	16
Norfolk Ho OX1	4
Norfolk St OX1	4
Norham Gdns OX2	11
Norham Mews OX2	11
Norham Rd OX2	11
Norman Smith Rd OX4	25
Normandy Cres OX4	21
Norreys Av OX1	19
Norreys Rd OX2	16
North Hinksey La OX2	10
North Hinksey Village OX2	18
North Manor Est OX44	26
North Oxford Bsns Centre OX5	3
North Parade Av OX2	11
North Pl OX3	13
North St OX2	4
North Way, Oxford OX3	12
North Way, Wolvercote OX2	8
Northern By-Pass, Oxford OX2	9
Northern By-Pass, Wolvercote OX2	8
Northfield Cl OX4	24
Northfield Rd OX3	13
Northampton Rd OX1	19
Northmoor Pl OX2	11
Northmoor Rd OX2	11
Norton Cl OX3	13
Nowell Rd OX4	24
Nuffield Rd OX3	21
Nunnery Cl OX4	25
Nurseries Rd OX5	6
Nursery Cl OX3	21
Nuthatch Cl OX4	25
Nye Bevin Cl OX4	20
Oak Dr OX5	7
Oakfield Ind Est OX8	27
Oakthorpe Pl OX2	11
Oakthorpe Rd OX2	11
Oasis Pk OX8	27
Oatlands Rd OX2	10
Observatory St OX2	11
Ockham Mews OX2	11
Old Barn Grnd OX3	21
Old Boars Hill OX1	22
Old Botley OX2	10
Old Chapel Cl OX5	7
Old Greyfriars St OX1	4
Old High St OX3	13
Old London Rd OX33	15
Old Marston Rd OX3	12
Old Nursery Vw OX1	23
Old Rd, Oxford OX3	20
Old Witney Rd OX8	27
Oliver Rd OX4	21
Orchard Cl, Oxford OX33	15
Orchard Cl, Witney OX8	27
Orchard La OX1	22
Orchard Rd OX2	11
Orchard Vw OX44	26
Orchard Way, Kidlington OX5	7
Orchard Way, Oxford OX4	24
Oriel Sq OX1	5
Oriel St OX1	5
Osberton Rd OX2	9
Osborne Cl, Kidlington OX5	6
Osborne Cl, Oxford OX2	8
Osler Rd OX3	13
Osney Ct OX2	10
Osney La OX1	4
Osney Mead OX3	4
Osney Mead Ind Est OX2	4

swestry Rd OX1	19 G4
tters Reach OX1	24 A3
useley Cl OX3	12 B4
utram OX4	20 C5
verbrook Gdns OX4	25 H2
verdale Cl OX3	13 F4
vermead Grn OX4	25 F2
wlington Cl OX2	10 A6
xenford Ho OX2	16 A6
xeye Ct OX4	25 F4
xford Bsns Centre OX1	4 B5
xford Bsns Pk OX2	9 E3
xford Bsns Pk North OX4	21 E5
xford Bsns Pk South OX4	21 E6
xford Ind Est OX5	6 C6
xford Motor Pk OX5	3 C6
xford Rd, Blackbird Leys OX4	25 G1
xford Rd, Cowley OX4	20 D4
xford Rd, Cumnor OX2	16 A5
xford Rd, Garsington OX44	26 A2
xford Rd, Horspath OX33	21 G5
xford Rd, Kennington OX1	23 E1
xford Rd, Kidlington OX5	7 E2
xford Rd, Littlemore OX4	24 C1
xford Rd, Marston OX3	12 A2
xford Rd, Witney OX8	27 C2
xford Rd, Woodstock OX20	3 B2
xford Retail Pk OX4	25 F1
xford Spires Bsns Pk OX5	3 C6
OX3	3 B2
xonian Pk OX5	6 C1
xpens Rd OX1	4 B5
addox Cl OX2	9 E5
aget Rd OX4	21 F5
almer Rd OX3	21 F1
aradise Sq OX1	4 C5
aradise St OX1	4 C4
ark Av OX5	6 D1
ark Cl, Oxford OX2	9 F3
ark Cl, Yarnton OX5	6 B6
ark End Pl OX1	4 B4
ark End St OX1	4 B4
ark Hill OX33	15 F3
ark La OX20	3 B2
ark St OX20	3 B2
ark Town OX2	11 F3
ark Way OX3	12 A1
arker Rd OX1	19 F4
arker St OX4	20 A4
arks Rd OX1	5 E1
arkside, Oxford OX44	26 F1
arkside, Woodstock OX20	3 C2
arkway Ct OX4	21 E6
arry Cl OX3	12 A5
arsons Pl OX4	20 B2
artridge Pl OX5	6 C2
artridge Walk OX4	25 H3
attison Pl OX4	24 B2
auling Rd OX3	21 F1
eacock Rd OX3	12 B5
eartree Cl OX4	25 G4
eat Moors OX3	21 E2
eel Pl OX1	19 H4
egasus Grange OX1	19 G2
egasus Rd OX4	25 F3
elican Pl OX3	27 C1
embroke Ct OX4	20 A2
embroke Sq OX1	5 E3
embroke St OX1	4 D5
ennycress Rd OX4	25 H2
ennyfarthing Pl OX1	4 D5
Pennywell Dr OX2	9 F3
Peppercorn Av OX3	21 F2
Percy St OX4	20 B4
Peregrine Rd OX4	25 E2
Periwinkle Pl OX4	25 G2
Perrin St OX3	13 E6
Peterley Rd OX4	21 G4
Pether Rd OX3	21 F1
Petre Pl OX5	7 F2
Pettiwell OX44	26 A4
Pheasant Walk OX4	24 B3
Phelps Pl*, Bath St OX4	20 A1
Phipps Rd OX4	21 E6
Phoebe Ct OX2	11 E1
Pickett Av OX3	21 F3
Pike Ter OX1	4 D5
Pimpernel Cl OX4	25 H2
Pine Cl, Blackbird Leys OX4	25 G1
Pine Cl, Garsington OX44	26 A2
Pink Hill La OX8	27 B3
Pinnocks Way OX2	16 C2
Piper St OX3	13 E6
Pipit Cl OX4	25 F3
Pipkin Way OX4	20 B4
Pitts Rd OX3	13 F5
Pixey Pl OX4	3 D2
Plane Tree Way OX20	3 D2
Plantation Rd OX2	11 E4
Plater Dr OX2	11 E3
Playfield Rd OX1	23 H4
Plough Cl OX2	8 C5
Ploughley Cl OX5	6 D3
Plover Dr OX4	25 F3
Pochard Pl OX4	25 G4
Polstead Rd OX2	11 E3
Pond Cl OX3	13 H5
Ponds La OX3	12 A2
Pony Rd OX4	21 G4
Pool Cl OX1	24 A5
Poplar Cl, Garsington OX44	26 A2
Poplar Cl, Kidlington OX5	7 E4
Poplar Gro OX1	24 A4
Poplar Rd OX2	10 A6
Portland Rd OX2	9 F6
Pottery Piece OX4	25 F3
Pottle Cl OX2	16 D1
Poulton Pl OX4	25 G1
Pound Cl OX5	6 B6
Pound Field Cl OX3	13 F3
Pound Way OX4	20 D6
Preachers La OX1	4 D6
Prestidge Pl OX5	7 F3
Prestwich Pl OX2	10 D6
Prichard Rd OX3	12 B5
Primrose Pl OX4	25 G3
Princes Ride OX20	3 C2
Princes St OX4	20 A2
Priors Forge OX2	9 F4
Priory Ct OX2	9 F4
Priory Rd OX4	24 D3
Prunus Cl OX4	25 G1
Pulker Cl OX4	20 D6
Pullens Fld OX3	12 B6
Pullens La OX3	12 C6
Purcell Rd OX3	12 A5
Purland Cl OX4	21 E5
Pusey La OX1	4 D2
Pusey St OX1	4 D2
Quarry End OX5	6 B2
Quarry High St OX3	13 F6
Quarry Hollow OX3	13 F6
Quarry Rd, Abingdon OX13	22 D5
Quarry Rd, Headington OX3	13 F6
Quartermain Cl OX4	20 B4
Queen St, Oxford OX1	4 D4
Queen St, Witney OX8	27 C2
Queens Av OX5	7 F3
Queens Cl, Oxford OX1	16 D2
Queens Cl, Witney OX8	27 C2
Queens La, Oxford OX1	5 F3
Queens La, Witney OX8	27 C2
Radcliffe Rd OX4	20 B5
Radcliffe Sq OX1	5 F3
Radford Cl OX4	24 B1
Rahere Rd OX4	24 D1
Railway La OX4	24 C2
Raleigh Park Rd OX2	18 B2
Rampion Cl OX4	25 H2
Ramsay Rd OX3	13 F5
Randolph St OX4	20 B3
Rawlinson Rd OX2	11 F2
Rawson Cl OX2	8 C4
Raymund Rd OX3	12 A3
Recreation Rd OX20	3 C2
Rectory La OX20	3 B2
Rectory Rd OX4	20 A2
Red Bridge Hollow OX1	19 G5
Red Copse La OX1	22 D2
Red Lion Sq OX1	4 D3
Rede Cl OX3	21 F2
Redland Rd OX3	12 C3
Redmoor Cl OX4	24 D3
Redwood Cl OX4	25 H2
Regent St OX4	20 A3
Remy Pl OX4	20 B6
Rest Harrow OX4	25 G2
Rewley Abbey Ct OX1	4 B3
Rewley Rd OX1	4 A2
Richard Gray Ct OX1	4 B5
Richards La OX2	9 E6
Richards Way OX3	13 G6
Richardson Ct*, Bath St OX4	20 A1
Richmond Rd OX1	4 B2
Rickyard Cl OX1	4 B3
Riddell Pl OX2	9 E4
Ridgefield Rd OX4	20 B3
Ridgemont Cl OX2	9 E6
Ridgeway OX1	22 A1
Ridgeway Rd OX3	13 G5
Ridley Rd OX4	21 F4
Rimmer Cl OX3	12 B3
Ringwood Rd OX3	13 H5
Rippington Dr OX3	12 A4
River Vw, Kennington OX1	24 A3
River Vw, Sandford-on-Thames OX4	24 B5
Rivermead Rd OX4	24 A1
Riverside Ct OX1	19 F1
Riverside Rd OX2	10 D6
Robert Robinson Av OX4	24 D3
Roberts Cl OX3	13 H4
Robin Pl OX4	25 F3
Robinson Cl OX1	5 E1
Robsart Pl OX2	16 A6
Rock Edge OX3	21 E1
Rock Farm La OX4	24 C4
Rockley Cotts OX13	17 A3
Roger Bacon La OX1	4 D5
Roger Dudman Way OX1	4 A1
Rogers St OX2	9 E6
Rolfe Pl OX3	12 B5
Roman Rd OX33	15 G5
Roman Way OX4	21 G5
Rookery Ho OX44	26 B3
Roosevelt Dr OX20	20 C1
Rosamund Dr OX20	3 A1
Rosamund Rd OX2	8 B4
Rose Gdns OX2	18 A1
Rose Hill OX4	20 D6
Rose La OX1	5 G5
Rose Pl OX1	4 D5
Rosemary Ct OX4	20 A3
Ross Ct OX1	23 H2
Rothafield Rd OX2	8 D4
Roundham Cl OX5	6 C2
Roundham Ct OX5	3 D6
Routh Rd OX3	13 G4
Rowan Cl OX5	7 E4
Rowan Gro OX3	25 H3
Rowel Dr OX5	6 B2
Rowland Cl OX2	8 B5
Rowland Hill Ct OX1	4 B5
Rowles Cl OX1	23 H2
Rowney Pl OX4	24 C1
Rupert Rd OX4	21 F4
Russell Ct OX2	
Russell St OX2	
Rutherway OX2	
Rutten La OX5	6 A4
Rutters Cl OX5	6 D2
Ryder Cl OX5	6 B4
Rymers La OX4	20 C4
Sadler Walk OX1	4 C6
Sadlers Cft OX44	26 B3
Sage Walk OX4	25 G3
St Aldates OX1	5 E4
St Andrews La OX3	13 E4
St Andrews Rd OX3	12 D4
St Andrews Sq OX20	3 A1
St Annes Rd OX3	13 E6
St Barnabas St OX2	4 B2
St Bernards Rd OX2	11 E4
St Catherines Ho*, Bath St OX4	20 A1
St Clements St OX4	5 H5
St Cross Rd OX1	5 G1
St Ebbes St OX1	4 D4
St Edwards Av OX2	9 E6
St Edwards Ct OX2	11 E1
St Francis Ct OX3	21 F3
St Georges Pl OX1	4 D3
St Giles OX1	4 D1
St Helens Pass OX1	5 F3
St John St OX1	4 C2
St Johns Dr OX5	7 E2
St Lawrence Rd OX3	19 F4
St Leonards Rd OX3	13 E6
St Lukes Rd OX4	21 E6
St Margarets Rd OX2	11 E3
St Martins Rd OX4	24 C1
St Marys Cl, Kidlington OX5	7 E1
St Marys Cl, Littlemore OX4	24 C2
St Marys Cl, Wheatley OX33	15 F4
St Marys Rd OX4	20 A2
St Michaels St OX1	4 D4
St Nicholas Rd OX4	24 C2
St Omer Rd OX4	20 D5
St Pauls Cres OX2	18 B1
St Peters Cl OX13	17 D6
St Peters Rd OX2	8 D5
St Swithuns Rd OX1	23 H3
St Thomas Mews OX1	4 C4
St Thomas St OX1	4 B4
Salegate La OX4	21 E5
Salesian Gdns OX4	21 E4
Salford Rd OX3	12 A4
Salisbury Cres OX2	9 E5
Salter Cl OX1	19 F2
Samphire Rd OX4	25 G2
Sanders Rd OX4	24 D3
Sandfield Rd OX3	12 C5
Sandford La OX1	24 A6
Sandford La Ind Est OX1	24 A6
Sandford Link Rd OX4	24 B2
Sandford Rd OX4	24 B3
Sandhill Rd OX5	6 A2
Sandleigh Rd OX13	17 C6
Sands Cl OX2	16 A5
Sandy La, Blackbird Leys OX4	25 F1
Sandy La, Boars Hill OX1	22 A2
Sandy La, Horspath OX33	14 B5
Sandy La, Kidlington OX5	6 A4
Sandy La West OX4	24 D2
Saunders Rd OX4	20 C4
Savile Rd OX1	5 F2
Sawpit Rd OX4	25 F1
Saxifrage Sq OX4	25 F3
Saxon Way OX3	12 C3
Scholar Pl OX2	16 D3
School Ct OX2	4 B1
School Pl OX1	19 G3
School Rd OX5	7 E2
Scott Cl OX5	6 D3
Scott Rd OX2	9 F5
Scrutton Cl OX3	13 F5
Seacourt Rd OX2	10 A6
Sefton Rd OX3	13 F5
Sermon Cl OX3	13 G6
She...	
Shelford...	
Shelley Cl OX...	
Shelley Rd OX4	
Shepherds Hill OX...	
Sheriffs Dr OX2	8 D...
Ship St OX1	5 E3
Shipton Rd OX20	3 C1
Shirelake Cl OX1	5 E6
Shirley Pl*, Juxon St OX2	11 E4
Shoe La OX1	4 D4
Shorte Cl OX3	21 G1
Shotover Kilns OX3	21 G1
Shotover Trading Est OX3	21 G1
Sibthorp Rd OX1	5 F1
Sidney St OX4	20 B3
Silkdale Cl OX4	21 E5
Silver Rd OX4	20 B3
Simons Cl OX33	15 F5
Simpsons Way OX1	23 H3
Skene Cl OX33	20 D1
Skylark Pl OX4	25 E3
Slade Cl OX3	21 F1
Slaymaker Cl OX3	13 G6
Snowdon Mede OX3	12 C4
Songers Cl OX2	16 D2
Sorrel Rd OX4	25 G2
South Av OX5	7 E5
South Bridge Row OX1	5 E6
South Cl OX5	7 F5
South Par OX2	9 E6
South Parks Rd OX1	5 E2
South St OX2	4 A5
Southcroft OX3	12 B2
Southdale Rd OX2	9 E4
Southend OX44	26 B3
Southern By-Pass Rd OX2	18 B1
Southfield Pk OX4	20 C2
Southfield Rd OX4	20 B3
Southmoor Pl OX2	11 E3
Southmoor Rd OX2	11 E4
Spareacre La OX8	27 B1
Sparrow Way OX4	25 G4
Sparsey Pl OX2	9 F4
Speedwell St OX1	4 D6
Spencer Av OX5	6 D6
Spencer Cres OX4	24 C1
Spencer Ct OX20	3 B2
Spindleberry Cl OX4	25 E3
Spindlers OX5	7 E1
Spinney Fld OX4	25 F3
Spooner Cl OX3	13 F5
Spring Copse OX1	19 F6
Spring La, Headington OX3	13 G6
Spring La, Horspath OX33	14 A6
Spring La, Littlemore OX4	25 E2
Springfield Rd, Kidlington OX5	7 F3
Springfield Rd, Oxford OX2	18 A1
Spruce Gdns OX4	25 F4
Spruce Rd OX5	7 E4
Squitchey La OX2	9 E5
Stable Cl OX1	4 B3
Stainer Pl OX3	12 A4
Stainfield Rd OX3	12 C3
Stanley Cl, Kidlington OX5	6 B4
Stanley Cl, Oxford OX2	18 B1
Stanley Rd OX4	20 A3
Stansfield Cl OX3	21 F1
Stansfield Pl OX3	21 F1
Stanton Rd OX2	18 B3
Stanville Rd OX2	16 D3
Stanway Rd OX3	13 G5
Stapleton Rd OX3	12 D6
Station App OX5	3 D6
Station Fld Ind Est OX5	3 D6
Station Rd, Oxford OX33	15 F5

[top-left corner torn; rotated text partially legible: Shakespeare Av OX4, Seventh Av OX3 … 21 G2, 20 B6, 13 G6, 13 F4]

27 C2
24 B2
11 E3
...n OX1 23 H2

Stin...
Stockl...
Stockmor... ...2
Stocks Tree ... B6
Stoke Pl OX2 ...2 D4
Stone Cl OX2 16 D1
Stone Mdw OX2 11 E2
Stone Quarry La OX4 20 B6
Stone St OX4 20 C2
Stones Ct*,
  St Clements St OX4 20 A2
Stonor Pl OX3 12 D6
Stoutsfield Cl OX5 6 A6
Stowford Rd OX3 13 G4
Stowood Cl OX3 13 F4
Stratfield Rd,
  Kidlington OX5 7 E5
Stratfield Rd,
  Oxford OX2 9 E6
Stratford Dr OX8 27 B1
Stratford St OX4 20 A3
Strawberry Path OX4 25 G3
Stubble Cl OX2 16 C2
Stubbs Av OX3 21 F3
Sturges Cl OX3 13 E3
Sugworth La OX14 23 G5
Summerfield OX1 19 G3
Summerfield Rd OX2 9 F6
Summerhill Rd OX2 9 E6
Summersgate OX2 9 E6
Sunderland Av OX2 8 D4
Sundew Cl OX4 25 H2
Sunningwell Rd,
  Abingdon OX13 22 C6
Sunningwell Rd,
  Oxford OX1 19 G4
Sunny Rise OX33 14 C6
Sunnymead Ct OX2 9 E4
Sunnyside,
  Cowley OX4 21 E5
Sunnyside,
  Wheatley OX33 15 G4
Sutton Rd OX3 12 C3
Swallow Cl OX4 25 G3
Swan Ct OX1 4 C5
Swan St,
  Oxford OX2 10 D6
Swan St, Witney OX8 27 B3
Sweetmans Rd OX2 18 B2
Swift Cl OX4 25 G3
Swinbourne Rd OX4 24 C2
Swinburne Rd OX4 20 A5
Sycamore Rd OX2 18 B2

Tackley Pl OX2 11 E3
Taggs Gate OX3 13 F3
Talbot Rd OX2 9 E3
Tanners La OX8 27 C2
Tarragon Dr OX4 25 G3
Taverner Pl OX3 12 A4
Tawney St OX4 20 B2
Teal Cl OX4 25 G4
Templar Rd OX4 9 E3
Templars Cl OX33 15 F4
Templars Retail Centre
  OX4 20 D5
Temple Ct OX4 20 D5
Temple Rd OX4 20 D4
Temple St OX4 20 A2
Tern Walk OX4 25 F4
Thackley End OX2 11 F2
Thames Ct OX8 27 C2
Thames St,
  Oxford OX1 4 C6

...ey OX33 15 H5
...eeches OX3 13 F4
...Bitterell OX8 27 C2
...e Boulevard OX3 3 C6
...he Broadway OX5 7 F5
The Causeway OX20 3 B2
The Cedars OX2 16 D3
The Closes OX5 7 E2
The Covert OX20 3 C2
The Crescent,
  Littlemore OX4 24 D4
The Crescent,
  Oxford OX2 11 E4
The Croft OX3 12 D5
The Devils Backbone
  OX1 19 F4
The Drive OX5 3 C6
The Field OX13 17 B6
The Garth,
  Kidlington OX5 6 B5
The Garth,
  Oxford OX2 18 B1
The Glebe,
  Cumnor OX2 16 A5
The Glebe,
  Wheatley OX33 15 F4
The Grates OX4 20 D6
The Green,
  Cuddesdon OX44 26 F2
The Green,
  Garsington OX44 26 B3
The Hamel OX1 4 C4
The Hill OX44 26 B3
The Homestead OX5 6 C2
The Lane OX44 26 F2
The Larches OX3 13 H5
The Ley OX20 3 C2
The Link,
  Headington OX3 13 G5
The Link,
  New Marston OX3 12 A4
The Links OX4 20 D4
The Moorlands OX5 7 E1
The Moors OX5 3 D6
The New Walk OX1 5 F5
The Old Bakery*,
  St Thomas St OX1 4 B4
The Old Tannery
  OX20 3 C2
The Oval OX4 24 B1
The Oxford
  Science Pk OX4 24 D4
The Paddock OX1 24 A5
The Paddocks OX5 6 B6
The Paddox OX2 9 E5
The Park OX4 16 A5
The Phelps OX5 6 D2
The Plain OX4 5 H5
The Quadrangle OX20 3 C1
The Ridings,
  Kidlington OX5 6 C1
The Ridings,
  Oxford OX3 21 G1
The Rookery OX5 6 D2
The Roundway OX3 13 G5
The Slade OX3 21 E1
The Spears OX5 6 A4
The Square OX8 27 C2
The Stables OX3 13 G6
The Triangle OX33 15 G4
The Tuer*,
  High St OX8 27 C2
The Willows OX1 17 C5
The Winnyards OX4 16 A6
Third Acre Rise OX2 16 D2
Thistle Dr OX4 25 H2
Thomson Ter OX4 24 B2
Thornbury Rd OX4 27 B2
Thorncliffe Rd OX2 11 E1

Thorne Cl OX5 6 C2
Three Corners Rd
  OX4 25 H2
Three Fields Rd OX3 21 F3
Thrift Pl OX4 25 G2
Tidmarsh La OX1 4 C4
Tilbury La OX2 10 A6
Tilehouse Cl OX3 13 F5
Tilgarsley Rd OX8 27 A1
Timothy Way OX4 25 G3
Titup Hall Dr OX3 21 F1
Toot Hill Butts OX3 13 F5
Tower Cres OX4 4 D4
Town Furze OX3 21 E3
Town Grn OX5 7 E2
Townsend Sq OX4 20 B5
Toynbee Cl OX4 18 A1
Trafford Rd OX3 13 F5
Transport Way OX4 25 G1
Tree La OX4 20 B6
Treeground Pl OX5 7 E3
Trefoil Pl OX4 25 H2
Trevor Pl OX4 20 D5
Trill Mill Ct OX1 5 E6
Trinity Pl OX4 20 A4
Trinity Rd OX3 13 F6
Trinity St OX1 4 C6
Troy Cl OX3 21 F3
Tucker Rd OX4 25 F1
Tudor Cl OX4 20 A6
Turl St OX1 5 E3
Turn Again La OX1 4 D5
Turner Ct OX4 21 E4
Turnpike Rd OX2 16 D4
Tyndale Pl OX33 15 H4
Tyndale Rd OX4 20 A2

Ulfgar Rd OX2 8 D5
Underhill Cres OX3 13 G4
Union St,
  Oxford OX4 20 A2
Union St,
  Woodstock OX20 3 B2
Upland Ct OX2 9 E4
Upland Park Rd OX2 9 E5
Upper Barr OX4 20 D6
Upper Brook Hill
  OX20 3 B2
Upper Fisher Row
  OX1 4 B3
Upper Rd OX1 19 H6
Upton Cl OX4 24 D2
Upway Rd OX3 12 D3

Valentia Rd OX3 12 D6
Valley Rd OX33 14 C6
Van Diemans La
  OX4 24 D1
Vanbrugh Cl OX20 3 B1
Varsity Pl OX4 19 G4
Venables Cl OX2 11 E4
Venneit Cl OX1 4 A1
Verbena Way OX4 25 F4
Vermont Dr OX20 3 A1
Vernon Av OX3 18 C3
Vetch Pl OX4 25 G2
Vicarage Cl OX4 24 C2
Vicarage Ct OX1 19 G3
Vicarage La OX1 19 G3
Vicarage Rd,
  Kidlington OX5 7 F2
Vicarage Rd,
  Oxford OX1 19 G3
Victor St OX2 4 B1
Victoria Ct OX1 4 D3
Victoria Rd OX2 9 F5
Villiers La OX4 20 C6
Violet Way OX4 25 F4

Walton Cres OX1 4 B2
Walton La OX1 4 C2
Walton Manor Ct OX2 11 E4
Walton St OX1,2 4 C1
Walton Well Rd OX2 11 E4
Warbler Walk OX4 25 F3
Warburg Cres OX4 25 G1

Warnborough Rd
  OX2 11 E3
Warneford La OX3 20 C1
Warneford Rd OX4 20 B2
Warren Cres OX3 21 E1
Warwick St OX4 20 A4
Water Eaton La OX5 7 G3
Water Eaton Rd OX2 9 F5
Watermans Reach*,
  Brook St OX1 19 G2
Watermead OX5 7 F2
Watermill Way OX3 13 H4
Watlington Rd OX4 25 G1
Watson Cres OX13 17 C5
Watts Way OX5 6 D2
Waverley Av OX5 7 F3
Wayfaring Cl OX4 25 F4
Waynflete Rd OX3 13 G4
Webbs Cl OX2 8 B5
Webbs Way OX5 7 F1
Weirs La OX1 19 H4
Weldon Rd OX3 12 A4
Wellington Pl OX1 4 D2
Wellington Sq OX1 4 C2
Wellington St OX2 4 B2
Wentworth Rd OX2 9 E5
Wern Rd OX2 9 F4
Wesley Cl OX4 25 F2
West Gro OX2 9 F5
West St OX2 11 E6
West Vw OX4 20 B6
West Way OX2 10 A6
Westbury Cres OX4 20 C6
Western By-Pass OX2 8 A6
Western Rd OX1 19 G2
Westfield Cl OX4 20 D4
Westfield Rd OX4 15 F4
Westgate Shopping
  Centre OX1 4 D5
Westland Way OX20 3 A1
Westlands Dr OX3 12 C3
Westminster Way
  OX2 10 B6
Westrup Cl OX3 12 A5
Westway Shopping
  Centre OX2 10 A6
Weyland Rd OX3 13 F6
Wharf Rd OX8 27 D3
Wharton Rd OX3 13 E5
Wheatley Rd OX44 26 B3
Wheatsheaf Yd OX1 5 E4
White Cross OX13 22 A6
White Hart OX3 12 A2
White Hill La OX1 17 C3
White Rd OX4 21 F5
White Way OX5 7 E3
Whitehouse Rd OX1 19 F2
Whitethorn Way OX4 25 F2
Whitson Pl OX4 20 B3
Whitworth Pl OX2 4 A1
Wick Cl OX4 13 F4
Wilberforce St OX3 13 E6
Wilcote Rd OX4 21 F5
Wilkins Rd OX4 21 E5
William Kimber Cres
  OX3 13 F5
William Orchard Cl
  OX3 13 E4
William St OX3 12 B6
Williamson Way OX4 24 B2
Willow Cl,
  Kidlington OX5 6 A5
Willow Cl,
  Oxford OX44 26 A2
Willow Way,
  Kidlington OX5 6 A2
Willow Way,
  Oxford OX4 25 F2
Willows Edge OX8 27 A2
Wilmots OX44 25 H6
Wilsdon Way OX5 6 C2
Wilson Pl*,
  Cave St OX4 20 A1
Winchester Rd OX2 11 F3
Windale Av OX4 25 F3
Windmill La OX33 14 D6

Windmill Rd OX3 13 ...
Windsor Cres OX3 12 A...
Windsor St OX3 13 ...
Wingate Cl OX4 25 ...
Wingfield St OX4 20 A...
Winston Cl OX5 7 ...
Wise Av OX5 6 D...
Witney Rd OX8 27 ...
Wolsey Ct OX5 3 A...
Wolsey Rd OX2 9 ...
Wolvercote Grn OX2 8 C...
Wood Farm Rd OX3 21 F...
Woodbine Pl OX1 4 E...
Woodcroft OX1 23 H...
Woodhouse Way
  OX4 20 E...
Woodlands OX5 7 F...
Woodlands Cl OX3 12 C...
Woodlands Cl OX3 12 C...
Woodpecker Grn
  OX4 25 G...
Woodruff Cl OX4 25 G...
Woodstock Cl OX2 8 D...
Woodstock Ct OX2 9 E...
Woodstock Rd,
  Kidlington OX5 3 A...
Woodstock Rd,
  Oxford OX2 4 D...
Woodstock Rd,
  Wolvercote OX2 8 C...
Woodstock Rd East
  OX5 3 A...
Wooten Dr OX4 20 B...
Wootton Bsns Pk
  OX13 17 C...
Worcester Pl OX1 4 C...
Worcester St OX1 4 C...
Wren Cl OX33 15 F...
Wrightson Cl OX33 14 B...
Wyatt Rd OX2 9 F...
Wychwood La OX3 13 H...
Wykeham Cres OX4 20 D...
Wylie Cl OX3 21 E...
Wynbush Rd OX4 24 B...
Wyndham Way OX2 8 D...
Wytham Cl OX4 27 C...
Wytham St OX1 19 G...
Wytham Vw OX8 27 C...

Yarnells Hill OX2 18 B...
Yarnells Rd OX2 18 B...
Yarnton Ct OX5 6 D...
Yarnton La OX5 6 C...
Yarnton Rd OX5 6 D...
Yarrow Cl OX4 25 F...
Yeats Cl OX4 21 F...
Yeftly Dr OX4 24 B...
Yew Cl OX4 25 H...
York Av OX3 21 F...
York Pl OX4 5 H...
York Rd OX3 13 F...